The Speaking and the *Speakers* of Literature

The Speaking and the *Speakers* of Literature

PAUL CAMPBELL

California State College at Los Angeles

Dickenson Publishing Company, Inc., Belmont, California

L.C. Cat. Card No. 66–28323
Printed in the United States of America

Acknowledgments

To Professor Donald Hargis, University of California at Los Angeles, and Professor Laura Chase, California State College at Los Angeles, for their help in the final stages of this book, and to Professor William McCoard, University of Southern California, in whose classes I was introduced to many of these ideas. I also wish to thank my publisher, The Macmillan Company, for permission to prepare this book for Dickenson Publishing Company.

"Blue Girls" (p. 24) by John Crowe Ransom. Copyright 1927 by Alfred A. Knopf, Inc. and renewed 1955 by John Crowe Ransom. Reprinted from *Selected Poems by John Crowe Ransom*, Revised Edition, by permission of the publisher.

"The Span of Life" (p. 29) and "The Lovely Shall Be Choosers" (pp. 120–21) by Robert Frost from *Complete Poems of Robert Frost*. Copyright 1928 by Holt, Rinehart and Winston, Inc. Copyright 1936 and 1956 by Robert Frost. Copyright 1964 by Lesley Frost Ballantine. Reprinted by permission of Holt, Rinehart and Winston, Inc.

"Ars Poetica" (pp. 30–31) by Archibald MacLeish from *Collected Poems, 1917–1952*, copyright 1952 by Archibald MacLeish, quoted by permission of Houghton Mifflin Company.

"Richard Cory" (pp. 41–42) is reprinted with the permission of Charles Scribner's Sons from *The Children of the Night* by Edwin Arlington Robinson.

"The Lady's Not for Burning" (pp. 46–47) by Christopher Fry quoted by permission of Oxford University Press, Inc.

"USA" (pp. 50–51) quoted by permission of Paul Engle and Random House, Inc.

"Snowy Heron" (p. 52) by John Ciardi, from *I Marry You* by John Ciardi. Copyright 1958 by Rutgers University Press, New Brunswick, N.J. Reprinted by permission of the author.

"Remembering Golden Bells" (pp. 59–60) by Po Chü-i, translated by Arthur Waley, from *Translations from the Chinese*. Reprinted by permission of Random House, Inc.

"An Old Man of Boulogne" (p. 68), anonymous, from *The Silver Treasury of Light Verse*, edited by Oscar Williams, copyright 1957, by permission of the Executors of the Estate of Oscar Williams.

"I Knew a Woman Lovely in Her Bones" (pp. 68–69) copyright 1954 by Theodore Roethke from the book *Words for the Wind* by Theodore Roethke. Reprinted by permission of Doubleday & Company, Inc. First appeared under the title "Poem" in *Harper's Bazaar* (Dec., 1954), p. 101.

"Exploration by Air," Part II (p. 70) by Fleming MacLeish quoted by permission of Duell, Sloan & Pearce, Inc.

"The Devil and Daniel Webster" (pp. 70–71) reprinted from *Selected Works of Stephen Vincent Benét*, Holt, Rinehart and Winston, Inc. Copyright 1936 by Curtis Publishing Company, renewed 1964 by Thomas C. Benét, Stephanie B. Mahin, and Rachel Benét Lewis. Reprinted by permission of Brandt & Brandt.

"Part of Plenty" (p. 72) from the book *Aegean Islands* by Bernard Spencer. Copyright 1946 by Bernard Spencer. Reprinted by permission of Doubleday & Company, Inc.

Excerpt from *Hawaii* (p. 86) by James Michener. Copyright 1959 by James A. Michener. Reprinted by permission of Random House, Inc.

"Mr. Flood's Party" (p. 88) reprinted with permission of The Macmillan Company from *Collected Poems* by Edwin Arlington Robinson. Copyright 1921 by Edwin Arlington Robinson, renewed 1949 by Ruth Nivison.

Lines from "The Great Lover" (pp. 88–89) by Rupert Brooke reprinted by permission of Dodd, Mead & Company, Inc. from *The Collected Poems of Rupert Brooke*, copyright 1915 by Dodd, Mead & Company, and 1943 by Edward Marsh.

"The Unknown Citizen" (pp. 91–92) by W. H. Auden. Copyright 1940 by W. H. Auden. Reprinted from *The Collected Poetry of W. H. Auden* by permission of Random House, Inc.

Red Jacket's speech (pp. 94–97) from *The World's Great Speeches*, Second Revised Edition, edited by Lewis Copeland and Lawrence W. Lamm. New York: Dover Publications, Inc., 1958. Copyright by Copeland & Lamm, Inc., and reprinted with their permission.

"Reuben Bright" (p. 99) is reprinted with permission of Charles Scribner's Sons from *The Children of the Night* by Edwin Arlington Robinson (1897).

"Quest" (pp. 100–101) by Edwin Honig, by permission of Edwin Honig, copyright 1959, from *The Gazabos: 41 Poems*, published by Clarke & Way, Inc., N.Y. First published in *Commonweal* (*NY*), May, 1942, under the title "In Quest To Have Not."

"Woman" (p. 106) from the *Shi-King* by Confucius, translated by H. A. Giles in *A History of Chinese Literature*. Reprinted by permission of Meredith Press.

"John Brown's Body" (pp. 107–111) from *Selected Works of Stephen Vincent Benét*, published by Holt, Rinehart & Winston. Copyright 1927, 1928 by Stephen Vincent Benét, renewed 1955 by Rosemary Carr Benét. Reprinted by permission of Brandt & Brandt.

"Without Ceremony" (p. 115) copyright 1958 by Vassar Miller. Reprinted from *Wage War on Silence*, by Vassar Miller, by permission of Wesleyan University Press.

"sweet spring is your" (pp. 138–39) by E. E. Cummings, copyright 1944 by E. E. Cummings. Reprinted from his volume *Poems 1923–1954* by permission of Harcourt, Brace & World, Inc.

"A Poet's Advice" (pp. 139–40) copyright 1955 by E. E. Cummings. Reprinted from *E. E. Cummings: A Miscellany* edited by George J. Firmage, by permission of Harcourt, Brace & World, Inc.

Preface

❦

IF you agree that the usual or conventional text in the area of oral interpretation is one that talks of interpretation as the act of performing literature for an audience, with considerable emphasis on the interpreter's use of his voice and body, you will find this book unusual and unconventional. Nothing in it is new. Much of what is in it is newly viewed, newly emphasized, and newly combined.

I see oral interpretation not as performance but as the process of *oralizing literature*. And it seems to me that in that process some very important things happen to the reader in relation to himself, in relation to the literature, and, finally, in relation to an actual audience, when there is one. I have tried to talk about these things that happen to the reader. The basic framework I have chosen—the who? what? when? where? and how? of literature—will be familiar to everybody in the field. Many of the things discussed under these headings will be less familiar. Some of them may seem a bit esoteric. I think they are. I also think they work.

The book will prove usable, I hope, on several levels and in several ways. It can be used as a basic text, supplemented by other books. It can be used as an auxiliary text, either as a means of going further in certain directions, or, perhaps, as a means of setting out opposing or contradictory points of view. As far as degree of difficulty is concerned, I have a personal prejudice. I think most beginning texts are far too elementary. This one seems to me to be simple enough to be used in most beginning courses in interpretation, but it also seems to me to be involved enough, convoluted enough, even abstruse enough, to be used in most advanced courses. I hope the book may make a few demands on teachers, most of whom, I believe, welcome those demands. After all, our own need to stretch is fully as important as that of our students.

Most of all, though, I hope the readers of this book will have fun with it—fun in trying out new ideas—fun in agreeing or disagreeing with my concepts—fun in disproving some or all of them—fun in having to come up with new answers—and, especially, fun in living with literature somewhat differently.

Paul Campbell

Contents

❈ CONTENTS ❈

The Speaking and the *Speakers* of Literature

Introduction

❦

Approaches to literature

IT IS possible to use the term *literature* to mean written language—any and all written language. Such a definition is an operational one, and is clear and understandable. It is not, however, very useful. Applying it, one is forced to state that a Shakespearean sonnet, a novel by Thomas Mann, a dirty limerick, a work on the philosophy of science, a billboard advertisement, the Bible, the Dead Sea Scrolls, the telephone directory, all textbooks, and street signs have some basic quality in common. They are, after all, written language. Obviously they share the fact or quality of being written language. But is that in any sense a basic or fundamental characteristic of these items? Does the limerick become literature only after its originator writes it down? If so, what is it prior to the writing? Is a poem literature only after its author puts it in writing? If so, what is it before that point? Is a story literature only after its teller puts it into visual form? If so, what is it when it is told orally?

It would seem that the limerick is a limerick, the poem a poem, and the story a story both before and after they are written down. Therefore, it would seem that the shared quality or characteristic that makes all these literature must be something other than the fact of being written. One might say that anything that is *capable* of being written is literature. But this simply compounds the problem. One might even go

1

so far as to say that any use of words, of language, written
or unwritten, is literature. At that point, one faces the complete idiocy of having to call a baby's "urgoo" and *War and
Peace* literature.

The answer seems to lie in the direction of narrowing, of
making more specific the definition of literature. The real
differences in the above list of items lie in the imaginativeness
with which the authors use language, and the impact that their
imaginations have on audiences.[1] Literature, in this narrower
sense, means language, written or unwritten, that is notable
for the expressiveness and imaginativeness of its content
and/or form, as opposed to language that is notable for its
technical content or erudition, or the more ephemeral language forms such as journalism. This, of course, is a rather
common definition of literature. It is found, in varying forms,
in practically all dictionaries.

Using this narrower definition, the Shakespearean sonnet,
the Thomas Mann novel, and the Bible are literature. The
others belong to various verbal arts or disciplines. Philosophy,
for instance, is philosophy, written or unwritten. Science is
science, etc. Clearly, there will be areas or works that are
difficult to classify neatly. A biography may belong to several
disciplines, literature among them.

Approaches to oral interpretation

Quite analogous to the above approaches to literature are
the possible approaches to oral interpretation. A cynical grad-
uate student, perhaps tired of the frequent attempts by writers
to define it, once described oral interpretation as "reading
with the mouth." In its broadest sense, oral interpretation
means reading aloud—reading aloud in any and all ways any
and all things. This, too, is a perfectly clear and understandable definition. And it, too, is not very useful. Applying it,
one finds that reading aloud the billboards from a passing
car, reading a Browning monologue so that the audience is
caught up in the drama of the piece, reading a business letter

to a colleague for purely factual reasons, reading aloud to oneself a scene from Lorca's *Blood Wedding* for the sheer joy of hearing one's voice and feeling one's body perform the material, and reading aloud an intricate piece of verse simply to understand more clearly the rhythms involved are all oral interpretation. In all these cases written words have been turned into oral words. But is that enough to make all these things basically similar? Is oral interpretation reading aloud—period?

Although many texts in Oral Interpretation include examples such as those given above, and some speak of the *practical* reasons for studying oral interpretation, the need to give committee reports, book reports, etc., it would seem that both in terms of the material performed and the intent of the performer, the above items differ enormously.[2] If one must make a book report to a class, or give a treasurer's report to a committee, one should have enough basic command of the language to be able to do so. However, it is difficult for this writer to see how a course—much less an academic area—on the college level can have such a goal.

More difficult to deal with, and, therefore, more dangerous, is the idea that oral interpretation is the performance of literature for an audience—a performance that is tastefully and rewardingly done (for the audience)—but a performance and nothing more.[3] It is in relation to this idea that writers have spent much time and effort, and some rather tortuous logic, defining oral interpretation in such a way as to differentiate it from acting. More will be said about this in Chapter Eight. For the present, it will simply be stated arbitrarily that if oral interpretation is solely, or even primarily, performance—performance *per se*—, if the only or the major goal of the oral interpreter is to read to an audience, then the differences, real or imaginary, that exist between interpretation and acting seem flimsy, indeed, as a foundation for an academic area, particularly on the college level.

What is left, then, as the proper domain of oral interpretation? Again, the analogy with literature is a workable one.

Oral interpretation, in the narrower sense, is the reading aloud of a literary work in a manner notable for its expressiveness and imaginativeness. This seems a simple enough statement, but it is easily misunderstood. As already stated, oral interpretation is not merely reading to an audience, no matter how excellently. The emphasis must be on the *reading aloud*, not simply reading aloud to an audience. It is the *oralization* of literature that is basic, not the performance before an audience.

In *The Well-Tempered Critic*, Northrop Frye says in the first chapter,

> Except for some aspects of scholarly research, dead languages have no place in education. But this does not commit us to making the simple-minded and ill-considered identification of dead languages with the Classical languages. A dead language is a language that one learns to read but never thinks of as spoken. What shows that it is dead is the third factor, the writing of the language. The professor of Latin does not think of Latin as a dead language except when he is marking students' proses. Similarly, a student who has learned to speak only associative jargon, will, when he tries to write English, find himself struggling with a language much more effectively dead than Julius Caesar. Good writing must be based on good speech; it will never come alive if it is based on reading alone.
>
> . . . Now if we write in a way that we never speak, the first thing that disappears is the rhythm. It is hardly possible to give any spring or bounce to words unless they come out of our own bodies and are, like dancing or singing, an expression of physical as well as mental energy. The second thing that disappears is the color. It is hardly possible to use vivid language unless one is seeing the imagery for oneself: even abstract words, if they are genuinely possessed by the person using them, will retain something of the concrete metaphor that they originally had. The third thing that disappears is the sense of personality, which only a basis in personal speech can

4

ever supply. These are all, as we have said, the results of a literary education centered in poetry. It is natural that associative speakers, for whom even English prose is a dead language, should regard English poetry with the baffled stare of a stranger accosted by a lunatic.[4]

Much has been said in these few words. And such a point of view is, naturally, entirely welcome to one in the field of Speech. The purpose of this text differs somewhat from that of Mr. Frye's book, but our areas of agreement are large. Indeed, his work should be required reading for all Speech majors.

The point, then, is that the narrow definitions of literature and of oral interpretation have much in common, and, in many ways, are interdependent. Mr. Frye focused on the achievement of a fuller ability to write the English language. This book is concerned with a fuller ability to read English literature. Oral language, or the oralization of language, or oral interpretation is basic to both.

Relationships between linguistic forms

Language exists as a concrete, an objective phenomenon only in the mouths and ears of individual speakers. All other linguistic forms are abstractions of this basic form, and the relationship between the abstracted form and the fundamental form frequently needs to be clarified and strengthened. Many of us fall too easily into the trap of considering such aspects of literature as rhythm, rhyme, alliteration, the transparency of language, etc., to be elements that are somehow inherent in the printed page. They are not. The printed word *symbolizes* the spoken word, and except for a few visual effects, typographical arrangement, etc., literature is a process of using one medium to symbolize another. It is much like writing a painting in words. One may describe the painting, perhaps symbolize it, but the words are still words, and the painting is still the painting.

The difference seems slight, or nonexistent, with written and spoken language because words are used in both cases. But the written word is related to its spoken counterpart only by purely arbitrary convention. Phoneticians are well aware of the fact that the visual sequence "dense," for example, is worlds away from the auditory sequence it symbolizes. They constantly go through the elementary step of pointing out that "dense" and "dents" are phonetically identical, and the more advanced step of making students aware that, in any syllable, to go from the sound [n] to the sound [s] necessitates the production of the sound [t]. We are almost entirely visually conditioned, and many of us find it difficult to listen objectively to sounds *per se*. Or, from another point of view, if one furiously screams the word "yes," is it the "same" word as a gently murmured "yes"? Certainly words have to do with meaning and its transfer. Certainly part or all of the meaning of a word is the response of hearers to that word. And certainly the responses to the two yeses will differ greatly. In what sense, then, are these two the "same" word? In the sense that the same visual symbols can be used to represent the word, and in that sense alone!

Abstraction and symbolization are necessary. Without these there could be no literature. But along with its pleasures, literature frequently brings pains in the form of difficult, or involved, or intricate passages. With both the pleasures and the pains, but especially with the pains, it is always helpful and often necessary to reverse the process of abstraction, to "translate" the written word into the spoken word.

There is much that can be and should be said *about* any worthwhile piece of literature. The reader must explore the work for himself, in addition to consulting the explorations of others. During this stage, the reader is speaking about the particular work. But there comes a point at which all that can profitably be said about the work has been said. At that point, the reader, if he is to achieve closer contact with the selection, must stop speaking *about* it and begin *speaking* it. John Ciardi points out that there is an important physiological basis of meaning. He says that the muscular feeling of a word is a basic part of its emotional feeling.[5] The special value of oral interpretation lies, not in the fact that it is a substitute for close analysis of literature, but in the fact that it can be used to go the one step further to reach such levels of feeling. That extra step is taken by responding to literature on a physical level that, in turn, leads to an emotional response. This is, of course, empathy, as it is experienced by the reader.

Much can and must be said about these lines from Macbeth:

> To-morrow, and to-morrow, and to-morrow,
> Creeps in this petty pace from day to day,
> To the last syllable of recorded time;
> And all our yesterdays have lighted fools
> The way to dusty death. Out, out, brief candle!
> Life's but a walking shadow; a poor player,
> That struts and frets his hour upon the stage,
> And then is heard no more: it is a tale
> Told by an idiot, full of sound and fury,
> Signifying nothing.

Eventually, however, the reader must speak the lines if he is to truly possess them. And at that point, issues arise that cannot be dealt with in any analytical sense. For instance, surely the repetitions of the word "to-morrow" are meant to suggest something of a creeping, petty pace. One way to suggest that deadly continuity of time would be to slur the sounds somewhat, running them together, as "to-morrow'n' to-morrow'n'to-morrow." But Shakespearean material is conventionally read with formal, crisp diction. The problem, then, if one is to observe this convention, is to produce all sounds clearly, particularly the [d] sounds in the two "and's." Can this be done, still reading the lines in a smooth legato to suggest the even and oppressive flow of time? Or would it be better to pause after each "to-morrow"? If so, would it be more effective to read each "to-morrow" with exactly the same inflection, pitch, and volume, or to read the second and third at progressively lower levels of energy and intensity? The first reading might suggest the crushing sameness of time, the second, the inevitable finality of death. Another question—how much of these first lines should be read on one breath? It is possible to read the three lines, down to "recorded time," on a single breath. Is that more effective than pausing for breath after the third "to-morrow," or after "pace," or after the second "day"?

These and other questions must be answered. In all probability, there is no single answer for all readers. The same reader may choose different answers at different times. The point is that the lines feel different to the reader depending on the performance techniques that he uses. And until he uses *some* techniques he will be unable to decide these matters. Obviously, it is not a question of the techniques governing the entire interpretation of this or any other selection. An intellectual analysis of this piece will make it obvious that it cannot be read in a light-hearted, chuckling fashion. By the time the reader hears his own voice and feels his own body performing the literature, he has already determined many aspects of his interpretation. His reaction to the material indicates certain techniques as being more appropriate than others. But when he actually uses those techniques, he will, very many times, try others to see if they do not work better. And in trying other techniques, he may very well change, in larger or smaller degree, his basic reaction to the material. It is a circular process. The reaction to the material may seem to determine the techniques used, but quite often working on techniques will change the reaction to the material.

The differences between these various techniques may appear slight. Indeed, each individual technique is a small thing. But in combination they are the stuff of creativity. It is by choosing among such slight differences that the reader goes beyond analysis and fully creates the work anew.

The reader as performer

The word "performance" has been used. In the process of changing the written word into the oral word, the reader becomes a performer. It is an inevitable step. The idea is not new. John Ciardi has said, "Above all else, poetry is a performance."[6] Melville Cane wrote, "I believe that poetry is primarily meant to be heard and should first of all be addressed to the ear, and is only secondarily meant to be read and for the eye."[7] Other writers put it somewhat differently, but the important element is the doing, the acting out, the performing of literature, all literature. A performer, however, performs for someone. A performance necessarily implies an audience. When the reader becomes a performer, he performs, firstly and most importantly, for himself. Or, to put it a little more schizophrenically, the performer part of the reader performs for the audience part of the reader.

For many years, actors have spoken of the sensation of standing off and watching themselves in performance, of observing themselves in the roles they play. It is a matter of keeping largely separate one's critical and creative faculties. And this is precisely what the reader-performer does. In doing so, the performer of a piece of material never really becomes the character(s) in the material. He pretends, but it is real pretense.

"Art" is more than coincidentally the first syllable of "artificial." As with all art, the reader is dealing with a combination of the real and the unreal. The feelings that the reader experiences are real feelings. As long as he accepts the fact of real feelings in an unreal context, he will appreciate and respond to literature. When he goes too far in either direction— feeling the entire process as real or unreal—he is lost. If he cannot accept and become a performer to an extent that will enable him to experience real emotional responses, literature will be an empty, worthless mass of scribbling. If he insists on total reality, he will necessarily limit himself to that literature with which he emotionally agrees, and even then he is likely to find reading a trying and tiring business.

Occasionally one sees performers who go too far toward total reality. Because of misdirected nervous energy (or is it emotional instability?) the rage, or despair, or grief is real. The audience, if there is one, immediately feels it as such, and the performance is ruined. There is no room left for illusion, for the emotional safety that audiences need.

Ordinary readers usually err in the other direction. They err because they do not thoroughly enough perform the literature for themselves. All sorts of forces operate to prevent such performance. One very simple one is the discomfort many of us feel at talking to ourselves, even in a completely private setting. Most of us do at times, but there remains the slight edge of worry at being caught and thought a bit odd. Yet the truly appreciative reader must frequently do just that—talk to himself. Often it is enough to talk silently, and this is not a contradiction in terms. There is considerable evidence to indicate that silent reading, or subvocal speech, is accompanied by many of the muscle movements involved in speaking aloud. Apparently, then, there is muscular or physiological meaning involved even in silent reading, *if* we let ourselves perform as we read. Scanning a page hurriedly is certainly not performance. Performance must involve pauses, changes in volume and pitch, etc., even if these are heard only in our mind's ear. But equally often, if not oftener, it must be an actual oral performance, even though it may be aimed at an audience of one—the reader. If the reader is to become a performer, he must perform for himself. He must do it because it is a way to get at many of the treasures of literature.

In other words, everything that is involved in the relationship between the reader and the performer, or the performer-part-of-the-reader and the audience-part-of-the-reader, is of basic importance whether or not the reader ever performs before an actual audience of other people. Oral interpretation has as its primary goal, not performance before an actual audience, but a quickened and deeper response to, and appreciation of, literature. The only audience *necessary* for such a response is the reader, himself.

The reader may, of course, perform for an audience of other listeners. When he does, the success or failure of that performance will depend largely on the earlier success or failure of the reader as he performs for himself.

The rest of this book is an attempt to show how one may approach literature as a performer, primarily a performer for that most exclusive, demanding, and rewarding of audiences, the reader, himself—secondarily a performer for actual audiences of other people.

CHAPTER ONE

The "who" of literature

❦

IT IS quite possible to take the view that literature is something separate and apart from people, to think of it as a group
of objects—novels, poems, short stories, etc. Much has been
said about the qualities inherent in these forms. And much of
what has been said has stemmed from a desire to escape the
difficulties of another, equally popular, point of view. That
other point of view holds that a literary selection is what its
author intends it to be, and that the reader must necessarily
understand the author as well as the work if he is to truly
comprehend the latter.

Many problems arise with this latter approach to literature.
What is one to do with selections by unknown authors? Or
with selections by authors about whom extremely little is
known? And what of selections that seem to many people
to mean far more, or far less, than the authors claim? Is it
then necessary to abandon all critical attitudes and simply
accept authors' statements about their works? To many
critics, these problems seem impossible to solve. And therefore, they take the stand that it is not the author but the work
itself that should be approached.[8] In general, they agree that
a literary work is not significant because its author claims
significance for it, but because the work itself affects people
in a significant way. Literary works are analyzed in great
detail and with much care. But because the works can be

"divorced" from the authors, it becomes possible to consider literature as a group of objects, and to analyze the characteristics of the classes into which these objects fall—poetry, plays, etc. And because the "person," the author, is removed from consideration, the approach can become basically impersonal and static.

In recent years, various writers have found that to think of a literary selection as a collection of items or characteristics leads to other problems. One can go so far as to count certain elements—words, vowels, short sentences, even punctuation marks—, but such "quantitative" analyses seem to say little about the magic of great literature. Indeed, one author may seem to use the same quantities of a particular element as another and yet create vastly superior or inferior works. Robert Frost and Edgar A. Guest both used very simple language in most of their writings, but few people would consider them equal in stature.

Since the basic problem seems to be the impersonal, non-dynamic approach to literature, the solution seems to be an approach that will make of literature a dynamic, moving, highly personal thing—a dramatic thing. And that brings us to a statement that is the basis of this book: *All literature is dramatic discourse.* Or, more simply, there is a fundamental sense in which all literature is drama.[9]

The "speaker"

As a starting point, let us begin with the "personal" quality of literature. Every literary work is a statement that could be appropriately uttered by some "person," some "speaker," or "speakers." For every piece of literature there is a speaker(s) whose personality and character are expressed by that piece of literature. With conventional drama, these speakers are the characters of the play, and though other literary forms present them less openly, there is behind, or imbedded in every piece of literature this same sort of speaker. This speaker is *not* a real person. He is created by the reader from clues presented by the author. If the work is considered as an expression of attitudes and feelings, then there must be some imaginary speaker who has those attitudes and feelings. And when the work is thought of as a statement by some speaker, it becomes a very "personal" thing. Perhaps it would be more accurate to consider it an "interpersonal" relationship between the reader and the speaker.

It is vitally important to realize that the speaker of a selection bears no *necessary* relationship to the actual author of that selection. If one were studying Hamlet's "To be, or not to be" soliloquy, it would be a fundamental mistake to assume that Hamlet was Shakespeare, that Shakespeare's character was somehow similar to Hamlet's. If this were true in any thoroughgoing sense, Shakespeare could have created only Hamlets. If one is to say that Shakespeare *was* Hamlet, one must add that he was also Lear, Pericles, Othello, Falstaff, Ophelia, etc. And to say that he was all of them is to say that he was no one of them.

When a particular author seems to use only one basic sort of speaker, it is, of course, a temptation to assume that the author *is*, in some way, that speaker. Even this, however, is a risky assumption. The author may be expressing only a tiny fraction of his personality through that speaker. He may be doing it for money, prestige, etc., and *not* because he *is* that speaker. Also, to assume that a given speaker *is* the author of a selection makes it impossible to deal with the fact that that author may produce works of widely varying quality. In one case, the speaker may be an insightful, imaginative person, in another, an absolute clod.

The speaker of a selection is not a real person. He is certainly not the author. Rather, he is an imaginary figure, *created* or *inferred* by the reader from the materials of the selection. The function of the speaker is to allow the reader to inter-act with the material in a dynamic, a dramatic fashion. When literature is peopled with speakers, the reader must then approach it in a very personal way, using quantitative measurements only as means to an end, never as the end itself.

Speakers of various sorts of literature

As an example, here is an excerpt from a piece of literature that would conventionally be called drama. It is the opening speech from Shakespeare's *King Richard III*.

> Now is the winter of our discontent
> Made glorious summer by this sun of York;
> And all the clouds that lowered upon our house
> In the deep bosom of the ocean buried.
> Now are our brows bound with victorious wreaths;
> Our bruised arms hung up for monuments;
> Our stern alarums chang'd to merry meetings,
> Our dreadful marches to delightful measures.
> Grim-visag'd war hath smooth'd his wrinkled front:
> And now,—instead of mounting barbed steeds
> To fright the souls of fearful adversaries,—
> He capers nimbly in a lady's chamber
> To the lascivious pleasing of a lute.
> But I,—that am not shap'd for sportive tricks,
> Nor made to court an amorous looking-glass;
> I, that am rudely stamp'd, and want love's majesty
> To strut before a wanton ambling nymph;
> I, that am curtail'd of this fair proportion,
> Cheated of feature by dissembling nature,
> Deform'd, unfinish'd, sent before my time
> Into this breathing world scarce half made up,
> And that so lamely and unfashionable
> That dogs bark at me as I halt by them;—
> Why, I, in this weak piping time of peace,
> Have no delight to pass away the time,
> Unless to spy my shadow in the sun,
> And descant on mine own deformity:
> And therefore,—since I cannot prove a lover,
> To entertain these fair well-spoken days,—
> I am determined to prove a villain,
> And hate the idle pleasures of these days.

These words are spoken by a character in the play, and we have no difficulty in assuming that these words are meant to be spoken by that character. Further, we assume that these words tell us something, perhaps a great deal, about that character, that speaker. Certainly we will know the speaker far better if we know the play, if we know all that the speaker says and does. But even in this short excerpt, the speaker tells us something about himself. He lets us see his anger, his hurt, his need for revenge against society or the fates.

The first lines seem direct enough. The speaker, Richard, is describing a time of peace. But underneath there is a controlled, bitter anger. That anger emerges openly when Richard begins to speak of his ugliness and deformity. Actually, it is not merely the anger that emerges, it is the speaker, Richard, himself. He describes himself and his feelings—"I, that am rudely stamped, . . . Cheated of feature by dissembling nature,/Deform'd, unfinish'd,"—and he clearly speaks his hurt, his misery, in the viciously sarcastic words, "Why, I, in this weak piping time of peace,/Have no delight to pass away the time,/Unless to spy my shadow in the sun,/And descant on mine own deformity." Here is a man who is deeply wounded by his physical ugliness, who masks his pain with anger, and who says clearly that he intends to lash out at those around him, to play the only part he can play—the villain.

All this, and more, we gather from these lines. Because we have seen this sort of literature actually performed in the theatre, and because we think of it as literature that is intended for performance, we react to it as a statement uttered by a speaker. Or, more accurately, we react to the speaker himself. We talk about Richard the person, not merely the opening monologue of the play.

Now consider the following selection. This is not conventional drama. Most of us are not used to finding speakers in this sort of material. But if we look, this speaker is no less real than the one in the above example.

HORSE SENSE
A horse can't pull while kicking.
This fact I merely mention.

17

And he can't kick while pulling,
Which is my chief contention.

Let's imitate the good old horse
And lead a life that's fitting;
Just pull an honest load, and then
There'll be no time for kicking.

—*Anonymous*

To begin with, the author of this piece is unknown. Therefore, there is no way to determine what he or she intended. (Also, it is impossible for my own remarks to get me into a lawsuit.) Conventionally, this selection could be discussed in terms of style, rhythm, tone, and any or all of a dozen other elements. And while it would undoubtedly be found wanting on those bases, it would be uncomfortably difficult to point out precisely why this is inferior to other seemingly similar selections. But if one considers this as dramatic discourse, if one attempts to discover the speaker behind it, several things are immediately apparent. First of all, the message. He pretty much lays his cards on the table. Don't complain so much, work harder, "pull an honest load," and the implication is clear enough: if you *are* complaining you're not pulling an honest load.

What can one say of such a speaker? What sort of person is he? For one thing, he apparently feels he has the right to *tell* us—not ask or suggest—he *tells*. There is a kind of boring cheer that covers the admonition, but it remains an admonition. And what sort of speaker could appropriately admonish in this fashion? One who, himself, griped instead of producing? If so, he's a hypocrite. One who didn't complain, but kept doing his very best? Even though the "movers and shakers" of the world rarely seem to take the time, or have the inclination, to advise the rest of us to follow their example, let's consider it a possibility. In the one case, then, the speaker is a person who is about and doing, and who makes it clear that the rest of us don't measure up to his standards; in the other case, he, like us, often complains overly much, but he neglects to include himself in that category. True, in the second stanza he says "let's," but the "let's" is like the nurse who wakes the patient and, with the same kind of cheer, asks if "we" are ready for "our" bath. The "we" and the "our" don't include the nurse, unless it's a very unusual hospital. And the "let's" doesn't really include the speaker of this selection. One reacts to the nurse and to this speaker in much the same way for much the same reasons. Who is this character who presumes, with this patronizing, two-faced cheerfulness, to *tell* me that I'm not "pulling an honest load"? It may very well be true, but I'm not likely to accept it without more sensitivity and insight than this speaker has displayed. Such is the probable reaction to this selection.

Notice that in a very real emotional sense this is an interpersonal reaction. It is a far cry from a statement about the overly regular metrical pattern, or the overly usual word choices involved. One is a person-thing relationship, the other a person-to-person, an interpersonal relationship.

Another example before getting involved in the ways one discovers the speaker of a selection. This excerpt is from a textbook in this field, Oral Interpretation, and it is from a part of the book in which the author is discussing the fact that all literature is dramatic discourse. Certainly we are not accustomed to finding speakers behind the stuff of textbooks. And often there are none. But consider this example:

> . . . accepting the literary text, be it play or poem, as essentially a dramatic form of discourse, we stress its experiential relations with the life it represents and the oral interpreter who expresses it.
>
> The modern statement of these relations goes something like this. There is the common experience of life itself, the life that wears you and me out, to our interest, our profit, and our misery. Then there is literature, a representation of some aspect of life. . . .[10]

Taken out of context, the thing loses much, of course. Still there is a speaker here. He is less apparent than in either of the previous examples. In other words, this excerpt is less obviously drama. It is, however, still basically dramatic in nature. This speaker is proposing a point of view. Primarily he is informing, rather than persuading, or trying to bring emotional pleasure. Yet in the middle of it all he says, "the life that wears you and me out, to our interest, our profit, and our misery." Why? That sentence could have gone, "There is the common experience of life itself." Period. We all know what life is, whatever it is. But the sentence didn't end there. And what sort of speaker would add what was added? Certainly one who *had* to do more than merely label it "life." One for whom life is richer, or more important, or more eerie. Then, he did not describe it in surging or turgid terms. Not "life that breaks us in ecstasy and lifts us in moments of hushed wonder." This "speaker" is far more controlled. The strongest word used is "misery." "Wears you and me out" sounds bitter or defeated when considered alone. But when followed by "to our interest, our profit, and our misery," it acquires multiple meanings, paradoxical meanings. So that this speaker feels life strongly—feels it as something complex, even contradictory—and, perhaps, feels its "misery" more than its "interest" or "profit." Putting it all together, this speaker is an intellectual, but a feeling, a tender intellectual.

Summary

It should be clear from the above examples that *what* the speaker says and what he leaves unsaid furnish the clues to his identity. The *what*, in other words, is the material from which the *who* is created. A careful investigation of the content of a selection is, therefore, basic to the understanding of the speaker. It is *not* a question of *substituting* the dramatistic approach used in this book for textual analysis. It *is* a question of combining the two, of creating a speaker out of the words that he speaks. It is at that point that literature becomes drama, and any approach to literature a dramatic act.

The next chapter will deal with the problem of analyzing *what* the speaker says.

CHAPTER TWO

The "what" of literature

❦

UNDERSTANDING, relating to, the speaker of a piece of literature, means that the reader must understand *what* the speaker
says, and at its simplest, understanding what the speaker says
requires an understanding of the words he uses. One must,
of course, know the historical or dictionary meanings of the
words used. This seems too obvious to mention. Nevertheless, this writer has heard students read material containing
words that were entirely unfamiliar to them. Such crimes
are intolerable because, too often, they indicate an attitude
on the part of the reader that goes something like, "Well,
the thing ought to be clear, and if it isn't, then it's the author's
fault for using those strange words." Authors have an obli-
gation to make their works understandable, but *not* to the
dolt who refuses to do the necessary work himself.

Words are symbols, not for things, but for the individual's
experience with those things. An unknown word is a symbol
for a thing, or some aspect of that thing, with which one
has had no experience. To know the word is to experience,
usually vicariously, the thing it symbolizes.

Heine, in describing a young virgin, said

> Her face is like a palimpsest—beneath the gothic lettering
> of the monk's sacred text lurks the pagan poet's half-
> effaced erotic verse.

21

"Palimpsest" is a rarely heard word, and the reader who refuses to become familiar with it will never be able to relate to the speaker behind these lines. The obvious inability to understand the excerpt is one thing, but worse still is the willingness to accept some murky idea of the word's meaning that may be furnished by the context. Never having heard the term, one could assume that it meant something about combining two images or qualities. But the reader who settles for that sort of "understanding" is committing literary suicide. "Palimpsest" means a parchment, tablet, or other writing material that has been used more than once, the earlier writings or engravings having been partially or wholly erased. The reader must know that definition. Without it he is lost. With it he can go on to deal with the excerpt in some detail. He can understand, for example, that the "earlier writings" are the sexual or sensuous nature of the girl, that the "monk's sacred text," the girl's religious training, has only partially erased "the pagan poet's . . . erotic verse"; that the speaker here may be condemning, to some extent, the girl (all girls?) because of this basic and ever present sensuality.

Contextual meaning

Somewhat more complicated than the above approach to words is the ability to deal with the word *as used*, the word in context. This, too, is essential for the reader. And two sorts of problems arise here. First, the context may exercise what can be called a "selective" function. That is, from a group of commonly understood meanings for a term, the context "chooses," "selects" an appropriate one. There is an Oriental proverb that says, "Lambs have the grace to suckle kneeling."[11] The key word here is "grace." Unlike "palimpsest," it is a commonly understood word. And any one of several meanings of "grace" will fit, at least approximately. "Pleasing or smooth movements," for instance. The saying makes sense using that meaning. But there is another meaning that is an exact, not an approximate, fit. It is "a sense of what is right." With that meaning, the proverb attains a symbolic power that is impossible with any other. The context, then, "selects" that meaning from the various available ones.

Quite often, understanding the word in context requires a familiarity with word history. The history or derivation of a word may not be a part of the obvious meaning with which one normally deals, but it is frequently necessary for a full appreciation of a particular selection. It is in connection with this level of meaning, as well as with others, that the issue of the author's intent, mentioned earlier, often arises. Critics such as W. K. Wimsatt, Jr., have argued against what they call the "intentional fallacy" with much success, and it is the position of this book that when there are bases for assuming that the speaker of a selection intends a fuller or richer meaning, such meaning in no way damages the author or the work.[12] And it does create a more powerful or insightful speaker with whom the reader may interact. Putting it differently, regardless of the author's intent, the speaker of a given selection always intends that the richest and most rewarding of meanings shall be understood. If one can choose between finding in a given selection multiple meanings that make the work memorable, and finding in it only the most pedestrian of meanings, there is no sense in which the reader can harm the work by making the former choice (assuming, of course, that valid bases exist for that choice).

This point is a crucial one. It is here that one hears the familiar objection, "But how do we know that the author meant all that?" Much of the time we know nothing at all of what the author intended. But is that any reason to assume that the author intended for the work to mean *nothing?* Of course not. And if sensitive, insightful readers find more in a particular selection than the author intended for them to find, is there any reason for saying that the work means *only* what the author intended and *no more?* If, like the Matterhorn, the meaning is there to be found, how can one say to a reader, "Now you must respond to this material only on certain levels—you must find it exciting and rewarding only within these limits—you must allow it to affect you only in specific ways and to a limited degree."

It seems to this writer that it is highly unlikely that many authors, especially the good ones, are *un*aware of the meanings involved in their works. It also seems totally impossible, at least in most instances, to prove that these authors *are aware* of the richly convoluted meanings that their works possess. And since to refuse to accept and respond to a piece of literature without proof that its author desired that acceptance and response is to discard many of the world's literary treasures, this text suggests the concept of the speaker, a concept that permits the enjoyment of those treasures.

Here is an example that requires and rewards a knowledge of word history:

BLUE GIRLS

Twirling your blue skirts, traveling the sward
Under the towers of your seminary,
Go listen to your teachers old and contrary
Without believing a word.

Tie the white fillets then about your lustrous hair
And think no more of what will come to pass
Than bluebirds that go walking on the grass
And chattering on the air.

Practice your beauty, blue girls, before it fail;
And I will cry with my loud lips and publish
Beauty which all our power shall never establish,
It is so frail.

For I could tell you a story which is true:
I know a lady with a terrible tongue,
Blear eyes fallen from blue,
All her perfections tarnished—yet it is not long
Since she was lovelier than any of you.

—*John Crowe Ransom*

John Ciardi in *How Does A Poem Mean?* discusses the word histories of some of the terms used here.[13] He points out the use of "traveling" in line 1 and "walking" in line 7. This is an especially rich example for the word-hungry reader. Part of the history of the word "travel" includes "travail"—to labor. In addition, then, to the obvious meaning of going from one place to another, the blue girls labor at the seminary. The bluebirds "walk," and part of the history of that word includes "to roll, revolve," "a rolling motion." A highly appropriate term to describe a bird's motion. But the important thing is the comparison that then becomes possible. The bluebirds "walk," with a rolling or revolving motion, and the blue girls "travel," labor, but do so "twirling" their skirts. "Twirl," to spin in a circular or revolving motion. The movement of the girls involves the same kind of motion.

Ciardi also points out the use of "practice" in line 9 and "perfections" in line 16, and says that since both terms derive from the root meaning "to do, to make," the girls (doing) and the woman (done), these word-histories bring into being a new level of comparison between the girls and the woman. Interestingly, he does not refer to the background of the word "practice" that includes "to bring about, to try to get, to plan, to plot." On this level, the girls are striving for their beauty, while the woman has lost hers. Or has she? Ciardi also ignores that part of the history of "tarnished" that means "hidden." In some sense, the woman's beauty is still present, though hidden. Ciardi also neglects the histories of "terrible" and "blear" that include "to flee," and "to deceive, to hoodwink," respectively. The woman has lost her friends or lovers because they have fled from her "terrible tongue" and deceiving "blear eyes."

The histories of words furnish important aspects of meaning in cases that are apparently quite simple. For instance, this selection probably seems entirely obvious to many readers:

Upon Julia's Clothes

When as in silks my Julia goes,
Then, then (me thinks) how sweetly flowes

That liquefaction of her clothes.
Next, when I cast mine eyes and see
That brave Vibration each way free;
O, how that glittering taketh me!
—*Robert Herrick*

The recurrence of words that suggest or depend on liquidity or water-like movement is unmistakable. "Flowes" and "liquefaction" are examples. But if one looks a bit deeper, other elements of meaning emerge. Julia's clothes *flowe*. This is the now obsolete spelling of *flow*. Flow means "to move in a manner suggesting a fluid." It also means "to glide along smoothly, without harshness or asperity." And it means "to have or be in abundance, to abound." Lastly, one of the rare meanings of the word is "to express one's feelings." All this, then, is involved in the simple word flow. Julia's clothes move in a fluid manner, smoothly, suggesting a richness or abundance (of the clothes, or Julia, or both?), and, perhaps, expressing some smooth, fluid, sensual feelings.

And Julia's clothes are of silk. Silk is a soft, flowing fabric. But is there anything else about silk that fits particularly well with flow? Well, silk is secreted by caterpillars as a viscous *fluid*. That may be a bit extreme, but think of the ways that cotton, wool, linen, etc., grow, and see if they combine well with *flow*. We are used to thinking of the word silk as a noun, but it is also a verb. As such, it means "to blossom." And what a perfect description of this Julia! She blossoms in silks. And the blossoming liquefies the silks.

Liquefaction is from the root word liquid. In turn, liquid derives from Latin root terms meaning "extended, prosperous, and water." Julia is dressed in rich, lustrous silks, and, perhaps, silks of subdued, quiet, watery colors.

In the next stanza *Vibration*, with a capital V, is one of the key words. It means "to swing, to move to and fro." It also means "to pulse, to throb." And one of the unusual meanings of the verb, to vibrate, is "to throw or cast." Moving to and fro, or pulsing and throbbing, can suggest a wave-like motion. But it is a *brave* vibration. Why *brave*? Among the seldom-used meanings of this word are "superior, excellent, fine, making a fine show or display, and to adorn." All these are appropriate elements of meaning for this context.

Julia's lover looks at her. He *casts* his eyes. One of the meanings of vibrate is "to cast." An interesting sort of mutuality. And he is taken by the *glittering*. Glitter means "to shine lustrously, to gleam." Water can gleam. But more important, there are common elements of meaning between *glitter* and *flow*, and between both of these and *brave*.

Finally, as an example of the sort of hidden meaning that can be found in the most ordinary-seeming places, consider the word *goes*. It means, for one thing, "self-originated movement," in contrast with more neutral verbs such as "move." Julia goes, and parts of Julia go, in a way that suggests independence, purpose. One of the root terms from which *go* is derived means "to reach, to overtake." Julia is, in this sense, a pursuer. She can overtake her lover.

All of these meanings, and similar ones, are in no sense substitutes for the more usual present-day meanings of words. They are additions to those familiar meanings, additions that bring new dimensions, new facets to the material. And the more dimensions of this sort the reader can find in the literature, the more exciting he makes it for himself.

The second of the two functions of the context referred to earlier is what this writer will call a "creative" function. In many cases, one may search vainly for a commonly understood meaning of a term that will fit a context. There may be none. It may be that in a very real sense the context "creates" a new meaning. For instance, in the lines from the opening speech of Richard III, "Now is the winter of our discontent/Made glorious summer by this sun of York," there are several terms for which conventional meanings do not suffice. "Winter of our discontent," for example, is nonsense if one insists on a traditional meaning for "winter." This is, of course, metaphorical language, and, as such, it is first of all literally untrue. There is no literal "winter" of "discontent."

But the phrase becomes meaningful, and powerfully so, because the context "creates" meaning by combining these terms in a new and special way. Both "winter" and "discontent," considered individually, are terms that are known to us, terms to which our experiences allow us to respond. As we have known them, however, there is nothing about "winter" that seems to match or combine with anything about "discontent." Here, in this context, the terms are combined in such a way as to make us aware that in this new, and special, and metaphorical sense there is something about "winter" that fits with something about "discontent." "Winter" is a season, a season of coldness, dreariness, perhaps. "Discontent" is, in a sense, the "cold season" of human emotions. Or, "winter" is the coldest, the worst part of this particular discontent. Or, "winter" is a recurrent season, and "discontent," then, a recurrent state—it is part of the human condition to be discontented. These, and other meanings, are created by the context.

A strong case can be made for the belief that all language begins as metaphorical language, and that, slowly, the metaphorical value erodes and is replaced by commonly understood, literally true meanings.[14] There are thousands of such examples at hand. "The river *ran* swiftly" probably functioned as a metaphor at one time. Today "run" does not mean leg-action of any sort. It simply means, in this context, to flow. "A chip on his shoulder," "down in the dumps," "a broken heart," "raining cats and dogs," "the telephone poles flew past the window," "head in the clouds," are further examples of metaphorical language that has been eroded into literally true language. (The word "eroded" in this paragraph is another example of the same thing.)

But with phrases like "soaring, silvery laughter," "the gentle touch of dusk," "fingers like deadly velvet," and "the soft weight of her love" the combinations are new, or new enough, for us to respond to that newness.

Similar to the metaphorical meaning created by the context, yet significantly different from it, is symbolic meaning that is also contextually created. Like metaphorical language, symbolism does not use literally true meanings, or rather uses them only partially. Unlike metaphor, symbolism does not combine terms in new ways. Instead, it uses words in conventional ways, but ways that involve two or more levels of meaning.[15] The following couplet by Robert Frost is an example:

> THE SPAN OF LIFE
> The old dog barks backward without getting up.
> I can remember when he was a pup.

On the surface, or factual, or literally true level, this is a simple statement about a dog who is old and tired, and an observer who remembers the dog's youth. But if that were all that was involved there would be little of value here. Certainly the thing would not be poetry. The fact is that, although the lines make sense on the literally true level, there is a surging symbolism here that goes far beyond (or below) the words. The dog is symbolic of man, the dog's short life of man's short life. The "I," the speaker, is aware of the shortness of human life, of his own life. And it is a painful awareness. The pain is calmly stated. It is not at all obvious. And it is possible to state it calmly because of the nature of symbolism. If the speaker of these lines had tried to describe his feelings about the brevity of life *directly*, he would have had to do so with intensity, or in dramatic terms, or, perhaps, with violence. Instead he described those feelings *indirectly*, in symbolism. Therefore, he could speak calmly and with restraint. On the surface level, he is talking about a dog, and intensity or violence would be out of place on that level. Only symbolically, with the words behind the words, is he talking about man and about himself. It is exactly this contradictory quality in symbolism that makes it effective. The sensitive reader will feel the strength of the emotions involved, and will feel the need for a strong expression of those emotions, but will also feel the restraint that the form (symbolism, in this case) imposes. It is as if the thing needed to be shouted or wept, but because of the demands of the art form, had to be uttered quietly.

With this particular example, and with many of Frost's works, the function of the speaker is of obvious and great importance. Frost frequently said of his works that they simply meant what they said—no more. Critics, however, have agreed that they do mean much more. Whether or not Frost intended for this, or any other selection, to mean what it means is of little importance from the point of view of this text. The speaker of this selection certainly intends the fullest meaning possible.

Here is one of the finest examples this writer knows of the use of metaphorical language and of symbolism. It is almost a textbook on the subject—a textbook that remains poetry:

ARS POETICA

A poem should be palpable and mute
As a globed fruit

Dumb
As old medallions to the thumb

Silent as the sleeve-worn stone
Of casement ledges where the moss has grown—

A poem should be wordless
As the flight of birds

A poem should be motionless in time
As the moon climbs

Leaving as the moon releases
Twig by twig the night-entangled trees,

Leaving, as the moon behind the winter leaves,
Memory by memory the mind—

A poem should be motionless in time
As the moon climbs

A poem should be equal to:
Not true

For all the history of grief
An empty doorway and a maple leaf

For love
The leaning grasses and two lights above the sea—
A poem should not mean
But be.

       —Archibald MacLeish

The first nine couplets are metaphors, the tenth and eleventh symbolism, and the twelfth metaphor. Notice that in the couplets that are metaphors the terms are combined in new ways. In the two couplets that are symbolism, there is no combination that is new. "For love the leaning grasses and two lights above the sea" means, on the surface level, just that: we will use as a symbol of love "the leaning grasses and two lights above the sea." Whether or not one understands the reasons for choosing this symbol, one can understand the fact that it was chosen. The symbolic level of meaning, of course, includes such things as the fact that "the leaning grasses" are made up of individual blades of grass that lean together under the wind's touch—much as two lovers "lean" together in sharing experiences—the fact that there are "two lights," not one—and "two lights above the sea"—lights that, perhaps, indicate a harbor, or place of safety—the fact that the sea itself is a common symbol for death, or being lost ("drowned") in fear or loneliness, and that love is a refuge from these things—and much, much more.

In contrast, "Palpable and mute as a globed fruit" (preceded by the implied words "a poem should be") is metaphor, and depends on new combinations of terms. Those combined are "poem" and "palpable," "poem" and "mute," and "globed fruit" and "mute." These are words that ordinarily do not go together. And in the next couplet, "Dumb as old medallions to the thumb" (again with the words "a poem should be" implied at the beginning), the new combinations are "poem" and "dumb," and "old medallions to the thumb" and "dumb." This is one of those perfectly right moments of poetry. "Dumb" is the key word. It means mute, unspeaking. How are "old medallions" "dumb" "to the thumb?" They are

31

smooth, worn with much handling. One can't feel the little ridges and indentations. The old medallion does not "speak" "to the thumb," to the tactile sense.

These kinds of contextual meaning are the stuff of poetry. Metaphor and symbolism are used in all sorts of literature, but when the meaning of a selection is dependent on and is expressed through metaphor and/or symbolism, that selection is poetry.

Over-all meaning

Finally, in addition to historical and contextual meanings, the reader must deal with the over-all meaning of the selection. And the whole is more than the sum of its parts. One cannot simply add up dictionary and contextual meanings and come out with an over-all meaning. Any piece of literature is *one* piece of literature. It is not a series of separate or unrelated items. Something exists (assuming the thing has some literary value) that makes for a oneness, a unity. The parts are inter-related in basic and important ways. The beginning is related to the ending and to the middle, and vice versa. As an example, consider these lines from the poem "Bannockburn" by Robert Burns:

> Scots, wha hae wi' Wallace bled,
> Scots, ham Bruce hae aften led,
> Welcome tae your gory bed!
> Or, tae victory!

Particularly if one knows the tune to which these words have been set, it is all too easy to regard them as a simple sort of folk ballad. The thing, however, is obviously a war cry, a call to battle. And it does not become that somewhere in the middle or toward the end. It starts with the word, "Scots." That first word must be related to the later words, "Welcome tae your gory bed." If that relation is to exist, "Scots" must mean more than "you people living in the geographical area called Scotland." And it does. It means "you people who live in this geographical area called Scotland, do not shame your proud heritage," or something to that effect. In other words, some hint of the "Welcome to your gory bed" meaning must be contained in, must be *predictable* because of the word "Scots." If it is not, the unity, the oneness of the piece is destroyed.

Over-all meaning, then, requires that words, phrases, sentences must make sense in relation to preceding and following words, phrases, and sentences. There is, of course, nothing new about that statement. It may, however, be useful to consider it from the somewhat unusual point of view based on the concept of "predictability."[16]

We predict the future on the basis of present and past clues. In terms of language, we predict future words on the basis of preceding words. The important point is that there are ties between these words. They are not separate little chunks of meaning. In so far as the grammatical structure of the language is concerned, this process is fairly obvious. For instance, let us say that there is to be a sequence of words, and that the first word is "the." Can one predict what word will occur next? Only within the broadest of limits. Certain words have been ruled out by that single symbol "the." We cannot say "the those," or "the these," or "the had," etc. Now let us say that the next word in the sequence is "horse." "The horse." At this point a far larger number of words has been excluded as possible successors. "The horse" cannot be followed ʰ "wall," "are," "workings," "warheads," etc., etc. Then, lᵉ increase the sequence by adding "is." "The horse is." one of many words may occur next. But compare number of words that might have followed "theʳ sibilities have dwindled drastically. Schematicalᴵ represented like this:

The   horse   is _____

| Number of words that might follow. |

Notice that, in a sense, "is" is contained in "the." On the basis of the single word "the," one could predict the *possibility* of the future occurrence of "is"; the *possible* future occurrence, not the *necessary* future occurrence. With the above example, "is" is contained in "the" along with many other possibilities. Those possibilities are fewer in number after the occurrence of "horse." Or, putting it differently, the word "is" has a certain degree of probability of future occurrence following "the," and a higher degree of probability following "horse."

Consider this longer sequence. "He gazed at the great piano." Given the one word "he," the future occurrence of the word "piano" is predictable, i.e., "piano," as a later word in the sequence, can be assigned a degree of probability. But with only "he" as an existing symbol, there are vast numbers of possible future word symbols. That is, "piano" has a very low degree of probability of future occurrence. When the word "gazed" is added, the picture changes. "He" might have been followed by a great many words, of which "gazed" is only one. And many of the words that might have followed "he" would not have led ultimately, to "piano," or, at least, would have led to "piano" only with difficulty and indirection. Try creating a short sequence beginning "he gritted," or "he swam," or "he choked," and ending with "piano." Following "he gazed," "piano" becomes more clearly predictable, more probable as a future word. "At" and "the" continue the process. The sequence might have gone "he gazed sleepily, swaying back and forth." But "he gazed at the" has to be followed soon by something at which one can gaze. "Piano," in other words, has become still more predictable, more probable as a succeeding symbol. "Great" adds to the specificity. Of the things at which he might have gazed, some are not "great." Those things are eliminated. Following the sequence "he gazed at the great," "piano" is by no means the only possible word. It is, however, far more probable, more predictable than it was when the sequence consisted of only "he."

Here are two other sequences. "The city seemed filled with

a gentle eagerness," and "the city seemed filled with a gentle pain." Considered from the point of view of rules of grammar, the same things that were said of the simpler sequences above may be said of these sequences. But looked at from the point of view of the semantic structure of language, some subtler and more important aspects of this concept of predictability become apparent. Semantically, any word that continues the thread or pattern of meaning qualifies as a succeeding symbol. The above sequences are meaningful. There are threads of meaning running through them. And those threads stretch *from the beginnings to the ends* of these sequences. The deceptive factor is that, although the last words in the sequences are different, the first seven words in each are the same. Or are they? *If* they are, then there can be no continuous threads of meaning involved. The first words, "The city," *cannot* be related to the last words, "eagerness" and "pain," if those words are considered as single entities. It is, of course, quite possible for the sequence to go "the city seemed filled with a gentle eagerness and pain." The first words, "the city," can be related to the final words "eagerness and pain," but that is a third choice. The sentence can end with "eagerness," or "pain," or "eagerness and pain." It cannot end with both the single word "eagerness" and the single word "pain."

The fact is, then, that the first seven words in the above sequences *are not the same* in terms of meaning. Schematically the sequences *cannot* be represented

$$\text{--------- The--city--seemed--filled--with--a--gentle} \begin{cases} \text{eagerness.} \\ \text{pain.} \end{cases}$$

with the dotted line symbolizing a thread of meaning. Rather they would be represented

$$\text{--------- The--city--seemed--filled--with--a--gentle--eagerness.}$$
$$\text{--------- The--city--seemed--filled--with--a--gentle--pain.}$$

35

with the dotted lines, the threads of meaning, beginning at slightly different points, and beginning immediately to separate, to diverge, so that they can arrive at the very different ends of "pain" and "eagerness." In visual form, the differences between these first seven words are far harder to perceive than in oral form. A person who read aloud the words "The city seemed filled with a gentle" *as if* they were to be followed by "eagerness," when, in fact, they were followed by "pain," would be reading poorly. With appropriate changes of inflection, tone, tempo, etc., a skilled reader would make it quite obvious that the above sequences were different, and would make those differences apparent long before he got to the last words. In this instance, of course, the differences involved are rather small. Nevertheless they *are* important—exceedingly so.

In visual form there are the same semantic differences between the first seven words in the sequences as there are in oral form, but one perceives and reacts to those differences differently. Assuming that one reads the sequences as isolated sentences, one becomes aware of the fact that the first seven words differ only as one reaches the eighth word. There is then, in the very brief time involved, a retroactive shifting or adjustment of meaning to allow all eight words to form a meaningful sequence.

It is with over-all meaning, especially, that the basic differences between written and oral language become apparent. The written word draws its meaning primarily from historical and contextual sources, and the over-all meaning of a piece of written language often becomes clear only retroactively, as indicated above. The oral word, however, draws meaning from two important additional sources, "voice" and "movement." "Voice" means any and all kinds of vocal variety, and "movement" means any and all sorts of physical behavior, from the broadest postural changes to the tiniest changes in facial expression. It is possible, therefore, by an appropriate use of voice and movement, to make oral sequences far more predictable than written ones. For instance, in the written sequence

Love you? Uh-huh. I love you with all the warmth and
tenderness that a convict loves his cell.

the pattern emerges only retroactively, after the last words.
But as oral language, some of the bitterness and sarcasm will
be clear in the first two words. The oral "love you" will
make the "convict loves his cell" more predictable than the
written "love you." (The speaker of a selection, then, is more
quickly and clearly revealed in oral language than in written
language. And it is the function of the oral reader to create
speakers who make the material as predictable as possible.)

As a further illustration, here is a longer and more involved
sequence. It is from Chapter 13 of Samuel Butler's *The Way
of All Flesh*.

> For some time the pair said nothing: what they must
> have felt during their first half-hour, the reader must
> guess, for it is beyond my power to tell him; at the end
> of that time, however, Theobald had rummaged up a
> conclusion from some odd corner of his soul to the ef-
> fect that now he and Christina were married the sooner
> they fell into their future mutual relations the better. If
> people who are in a difficulty will only do the first little
> reasonable thing which they can clearly recognize as rea-
> sonable, they will always find the next step more easy
> both to see and take. What, then, thought Theobald, was
> here at this moment the first and most obvious matter to
> be considered, and what would be an equitable view of
> his and Christina's relative positions in respect to it?
> Clearly their first dinner was their first joint entry into
> the duties and pleasures of married life. No less clearly
> it was Christina's duty to order it, and his own to eat
> it and pay for it.
> The arguments leading to this conclusion, and the con-
> clusion itself, flashed upon Theobald about three and a
> half miles after he had left Crampsford on the road to
> Newmarket. He had breakfasted early, but his usual ap-
> petite had failed him. They had left the vicarage at noon
> without staying for the wedding-breakfast. Theobald

liked an early dinner; it dawned upon him that he was beginning to be hungry; from this to the conclusion stated in the preceding paragraph the steps had been easy. After a few minutes' further reflection he broached the matter to his bride, and thus the ice was broken.

Mrs. Theobald was not prepared for so sudden an assumption of importance. Her nerves, never of the strongest, had been strung to their highest tension by the event of the morning. She wanted to escape observation; she was conscious of looking a little older than she quite liked to look as a bride who had been married that morning; she feared the landlady, the chambermaid, the waiter—everybody and everything; her heart beat so fast that she could hardly speak, much less go through the ordeal of ordering dinner in a strange hotel with a strange landlady. She begged and prayed to be let off. If Theobald would only order his dinner this once, she would order it any day and every day in the future.

But the inexorable Theobald was not to be put off with such absurd excuses. He was master now. Had not Christina less than two hours ago promised solemnly to honour and obey him, and was she turning restive over such a trifle as this? The loving smile departed from his face, and was succeeded by a scowl which that old Turk, his father, might have envied. "Stuff and nonsense, my dearest Christina," he exclaimed mildly, and stamped his foot upon the floor of the carriage. "It is a wife's duty to order her husband's dinner; you are my wife, and I shall expect you to order mine." Theobald was nothing if he was not logical.

The bride began to cry, and said he was unkind; whereon he said nothing, but revolved unutterable things in his heart. Was this, then, the end of his six years of unflagging devotion? Was it for this that when Christina had offered to let him off he had stuck to his engagement? Was this the outcome of her talks about duty and spiritual-mindedness—that now upon the very day of her marriage she should fail to see that the first step in obedience to God lay in obedience to himself? He would drive back to Crampsford; he would complain to Mr.

and Mrs. Allaby; he didn't mean to have married Christina; he hadn't married her; it was all a hideous dream; he would—But a voice kept ringing in his ears which said: "YOU CAN'T, CAN'T, CAN'T."

"CAN'T I?" screamed the unhappy creature to himself.

"NO," said the remorseless voice, "YOU CAN'T. YOU ARE A MARRIED MAN."

He rolled back in his corner of the carriage and for the first time felt how iniquitous were the marriage laws of England.

Dealing with excerpts from novels is dangerous in that what is true of the excerpt need not be true of the novel as a whole. The safest approach is to regard the excerpt as a work in its own right, and to consider that assumptions based on the excerpt apply to the entire novel only very tentatively. The above selection can be treated fairly easily as an isolated work, but statements about it may or may not be applicable to the complete novel.

In this selection, there is a smooth, steady progression from the neutral point of view taken at the very beginning to the satirical and deeply sarcastic attitude expressed at the end. Probably the first clue comes with the words, "Theobald had rummaged up a conclusion from some odd corner of his soul." To "rummage up a conclusion" is not a particularly flattering description of a mental process, and "some odd corner of his soul" seems to indicate that Theobald's interior rather resembled a junk shop. The speaker of the piece is already letting us know that he does not think too highly of Mr. Theobald. But, as yet, we don't know why. A sensitive oral reader, however, will not fail to make the note of wry humor quite clear, and, thereby, will make predictable the further development of this attitude.

The next few lines picture Theobald as a logical man. It is a pedestrian, unimaginative sort of logic, and it is certainly a far cry from the tenderness and absorption in his bride that we might expect from a just-married man. Again, the oral reader will make this clear. He might do it by exaggerating in his reading the "reasonableness," the "justice" of Theobald's viewpoint.

In the next paragraph there is a key sentence: "Theobald liked an early dinner; it dawned upon him that he was beginning to be hungry; from this to the conclusion stated in the preceding paragraph the steps had been easy." The speaker's thrusts are becoming a bit more vicious. He shows us Theobald reacting to his appetite, and reacting in an almost simian fashion—"it dawned upon him that he was beginning to be hungry"—almost as if he were discovering some significant concept in his own hunger. The oral reader will certainly emphasize these words, and the entire paragraph, and may do so in a drippingly sarcastic manner.

The speaker then focuses on Mrs. Theobald, and the attitude expressed is quite different. There is no sarcasm, no satire. She is shown as a nervous, uneasy, and, perhaps, slightly pathetic woman. Once more, the oral reader must make this attitude predictable. In the written words, the attitude emerges retroactively, probably with the description "she was conscious of looking a little older than she quite liked to look as a bride." But in oral language, the first sentence of the paragraph must make it plain that there has been a change in viewpoint. This sentence, and those that follow, will be read without sarcasm, more gently than what has gone before, even compassionately.

Then back to Theobald, a Theobald who is "not to be put off with such absurd excuses," absurd meaning anything that does not agree with his own ideas, and especially anything that is full of feeling instead of logic. By this time the speaker has made it quite clear that he is pitilessly dissecting Theobald, and the oral reader does not have to emphasize that attitude further. Instead, he must prepare for the crowning satire with which the selection ends. From here on the speaker *pretends* to take Theobald's side, to see things through his emotional eyes, and they are righteous eyes, indeed. The world, the fates have wronged poor Theobald. This ungrateful woman denies him, thwarts him. That incredible, criminal blindness of hers—to "fail to see that the first step in obedience to God lay in obedience to himself!" And, finally, the realization of the terrible trap into which he had fallen—the iniquitous marriage laws of England. With all this the oral reader must drop most of the savage satire, retaining and blending just enough of it with the pretended sincerity to create the quiet but happily vicious humour that ends the piece. By the time he gets to "he said nothing, but revolved unutterable things in his heart," the oral reader will have made fairly apparent this final attitude, and will have increased the predictability of the bleakly humorous ending. Actually, of course, the *implicit* satire increases throughout the selection, culminating with the final short paragraph. But the satire is made apparent by *explicitly* understating, pretending to be sincere in adopting Theobald's frame of reference. And it is here that the oral reader has the advantage of voice and movement. He can make this basic attitude, which is expressed through a complex of seemingly conflicting attitudes, clearer, more predictable than can the silent reader. He can say, for instance, "YOU ARE A MARRIED MAN," and say it with a mixture of Theobald's despair and the speaker's disdain.

The above examples have been ones in which there was a predictable thread of meaning running *throughout* the sequences. This is not always the case, of course. At times, authors deliberately disrupt meaning patterns, or make impossible continuous predictability. In the following selection, one cannot predict the ending from what precedes it.

RICHARD CORY

Whenever Richard Cory went down town,
    We people on the pavement looked at him;
He was a gentleman from sole to crown,
    Clean favored, and imperially slim.

And he was always quietly arrayed,
    And he was always human when he talked;

41

But still he fluttered pulses when he said,
   "Good morning," and he glittered when he walked.

And he was rich—yes, richer than a king—
   And admirably schooled in every grace:
In fine, we thought that he was everything
   To make us wish that we were in his place.

So on we worked and waited for the light,
   And went without the meat, and cursed the bread;
And Richard Cory, one calm summer night,
   Went home and put a bullet through his head.
                                    —*Edwin Arlington Robinson*

This becomes quite obvious when the poem is read aloud. Trying to read it ominously, in such a way as to make predictable the ending, simply destroys the selection. There is nothing ominous or foreboding about "he was a gentleman from sole to crown," or "clean-favored and imperially slim," or "fluttered pulses when he said 'Good morning'." The surprising and shocking ending, deliberately planned by the author, depends for its surprise and shock on the fact that it is not predictable.

With such selections, the reader, of course, must play the author's game and make the audience predict an ending other than the one that actually occurs. In other words, the reader pushes the predictability as far as possible. In most cases there is a continuous thread of predictability running through the material. In some there is not.

A sample analysis for meaning

In an attempt to illustrate these levels or kinds of meaning, here is an analysis of the opening paragraph of Dickens' *Tale of Two Cities*:

It was the best of times, it was the worst of times, it was the age of wisdom, it was the age of foolishness, it was the epoch of belief, it was the epoch of incredulity, it was the season of Light, it was the season of Darkness, it was the Spring of hope, it was the Winter of despair, we had everything before us, we had nothing before us, we were all going direct to Heaven, we were all going direct the other way—in short, the period was so far like the present period that some of its noisiest authorities insisted on its being received, for good or for evil, in the superlative degree of comparison only.

It is a paragraph and a sentence—a sentence made up of short phrases. What happens, basically, is that an attitude is made apparent, an attitude similar in certain ways to that of the excerpt from *The Way of All Flesh*.

At first a rather neutral point of view seems to have been taken. The words "best of times" and "worst of times" don't seem to involve any particularly strong feeling. The following "age of wisdom" and "age of foolishness" change the tone just a bit. "Age of wisdom" indicates a mellowness and an intellectual tranquility that the speaker of this selection must feel a little more strongly about than he does about "best of times." And the attitude toward an "age of foolishness" is certainly a little different from the feeling about the "worst of times;" "age of foolishness" is somewhat softer and considerably more personal.

The change continues with "epoch of belief" and "epoch of incredulity." There is a slightly stronger feeling to "epoch" than there is to "age." Webster says "age" refers to "a period of time in the life of mankind that has distinct but undateable boundaries"; "epoch" refers to "a period of time marked by some notable or monumental event." "Epoch of belief," then, means something more specific, though still unnamed, than "age of wisdom"—something more specific and more stirring. And "epoch of incredulity" implies more intensity and, perhaps, pain than "age of foolishness."

Next, "season of Light" and "season of Darkness," capital "L" and "D". Three things happen here. There is still more specificity—"age"—"epoch"—"season." Season implies a shorter time period. But it also implies a recurring period. "Light," then, comes (to man) seasonally. And the progression from "best" to "wisdom" to "belief" to "Light," and from "worst" to "foolishness" to "incredulity" to "Darkness," adds another level of strength and intensity. A slightly dramatic note seems to enter with the capitalized "Light" and "Darkness"—not "light" and "darkness," but "Light" and "Darkness."

"Winter of despair" and "Spring of hope" push the attitude more clearly into the open and into areas of feeling. A case can be made for considering the two previous phrases as metaphor, but these are the first two that are undoubtedly metaphorical (though some of the metaphorical value has eroded away with use). This is the first instance of different time-terms being used for the good and bad aspects of the thing. "Winter" and "Spring" are specifics, specific seasons. And, if you will, specific seasons of epochs of ages of times. "Despair" and "hope" are completely personal, completely human feelings as opposed to "Light"–"Darkness" and "belief"–"incredulity," which imply a generalized almost nonpersonal sort of feeling.

"We had everything before us, we had nothing before us" is a turning point, a qualitative change. The attitude, and the extremity of the contrasts involved, has become strong enough and intimate enough to require, for the first time, a personal pronoun—"we." "It" no longer suffices. The attitude can only be expressed by an overtly stated personal viewpoint.

"We were all going direct to Heaven, we were all going direct the other way" continues and intensifies the "we-ness" of the attitude. But an odd thing happens here. "We were all going direct the other way" somehow introduces a very slight note of—at least lightness, if not humor. If the word had been used—"we were all going direct to Hell"—it would have been quite different. As it is, there is almost a slight preparation—for what?

44

For an almost entirely unexpected change. So far the thing has been building. The attitude has seemed to become increasingly clear. A feeling of increasing involvement in the pleasure and pain of the "times"—"age"—"epoch"—"season" —"spring-winter." We expect an openly passionate comment to come along soon, or we would have expected it if it hadn't been for that "we were all going direct the other way." And instead of passion comes detachment, irony, amusement at the extent of man's blindness and incredible egotism. This period of time, described in the most extreme terms, would seem to have been a period unique in human history. But it is just the reverse—that period was like the present—and, therefore, everything that was said about that period applies to the present.

Finally, the piece comes almost full circle by dropping entirely the sweeping, singing phrases and describing people instead of periods. "Noisiest authorities," blind to any sense of history are exposed with gentle contempt for the hopelessly human failures that they are.

There is the attitude, at last. An attitude of compassion, of tenderness, of warmth, and of fear, of dismay, of revulsion, but also of humanely malign detachment.

An attitude toward analysis

One last point in this section on meaning. An attitude is frequently expressed that goes something like this. "I like literature, especially certain kinds of literature. And I respond to it strongly. I can sometimes lose myself pretty completely in a poem or play or novel. But if I start to analyze it, to break it up into some kind of artificial elements, I ruin it. The thing crumbles and loses its power and magic. So, I, personally, don't want to dissect literature, and frankly, I don't see any need for an analytic approach. It's enough for me to feel what I feel about it."

When this attitude really conceals the more basic one of

simply wanting to avoid the work involved in analysis, it, of course, deserves shock treatment of one sort or another. But when it is meant sincerely, and that is often the case, it must be respected. It has been this writer's experience that it does little good in these cases to point out the constructive and rewarding aspects of analysis.

There is, however, an attitude or approach to literature that is often useful for such readers. It is an approach that is analogous to "testing behavior" as the psychologists define it. "Testing behavior" is any behavior that attempts to discover the rules or limits or reality in one's environment. Children test their parents to see how much they can get away with, to see how dependable parental responses are. Adults test each other for much the same reasons—to see whether or not the love or anger or indifference is real. And one may test literature in basically the same fashion. (It's a moot point as to whether one is testing the literature or one's self.) One may try the particular piece to see if it is worthy, almost as if one were testing the worthiness of an opponent. Certainly there is a kind of magic and splendor in any good piece of literature. And if those qualities fall apart in the face of an analytic attack, it's doubtful that they were real to begin with. On the other hand, if one analyzes the thing in much detail and finds that it still holds together, that it refuses to be completely analyzed, that it keeps its splendor despite the reader's best efforts, one is likely to appreciate and respond more deeply than ever.

It is, in a sense, pitting the analytic "evil" in one's self against the literary or poetic "good" of the given selection.

For example, here is an excerpt from Christopher Fry's play *The Lady's Not For Burning* that has easily and with much grace resisted this writer's most determined efforts to "destroy" it.

> What is deep as love is deep, I'll have
> Deeply. What is good as love is good,
> I'll have well. Then if time and space

Have any purpose, I shall belong to it.
If not, if all is a pretty fiction
To distract the cherubim and seraphim
Who so continually do cry, the least
I can do is fill the curled shell of the world
With human deep-sea sound, and hold it to
The ear of God, until he has appetite
To taste our salt sorrow on his lips.

The speaker of these lines, the character in the play, is a girl
who is describing herself, her needs and desires. The first four
lines constitute a pretty straightforward statement, a statement that *is* analyzable. But the next seven lines are a different
matter. One can say much about them and say it profitably.
For instance, why "cherubim and seraphim?" Why not
"angels?" According to mythology or religious folklore,
there is a celestial hierarchy, and the cherubim and seraphim
are not ordinary angels, but rank next to God. Then there is
the fascinating and truly poetic relationship between the fact
that the cherubim and seraphim "do cry," apparently for man,
and the fact that the speaker hopes that "our salt sorrow,"
our tears, will be more meaningful to God than those of his
own highest angels. It is a protest, then, and a strong one.
And there is much, much more that these lines will yield to
the analyst.

But, there comes a point when, with all that can be said
about this excerpt, one realizes that there are depths of
mystery and beauty in these words that are impregnable. At
that point one returns, as it were, to the selection itself—a
selection made richer by the analyses used—and realizes with
much comfort that the one possible way to say what was said
is by using the poet's own words. They cannot be "translated"
or paraphrased without changing them, and changing them
drastically. The testing has disclosed very firm poetic
limits.

It is this writer's belief that any fine piece of literature will
withstand the testing of the analyst with similar success and
will be the more rewarding as a result.

Summary

Having created a speaker and analyzed what that speaker says, the reader must complete the picture by dealing with other dramatic elements of literature. Until he does so he will find the dramatistic approach offered here unworkable. Speakers neither exist nor speak in a void. They live in much the same multidimensional world that authors and readers inhabit. The next two chapters discuss the dimensions of that world.

CHAPTER THREE

The "where" and "when" of literature

❧

IN ADDITION to the "who" and "what" (the speaker and his message) of a selection, there are other dramatic elements that are present in varying degrees of clarity and specificity. They can be represented by the questions "where?" and "when?" As with the first two elements, it is in writing specifically for the theater that these factors are most apparent. In plays, the speaker, the character, is openly presented; by appropriate use of voice and movement, he makes his message as clear, as predictable, as possible; *and* he exists at a point, usually a very specific one, in time and space. Though these last two qualities are less clearly delineated in other literary forms, they are nevertheless present.

The "where"

The scene or setting of a work is dramatically important, not so much as an isolated element, but as a phase of the speaker himself. One is not the same person driving along an empty highway that one is arguing with an employer. We all play various roles at various times, and one of the things that determines a particular role is the place in which we find ourselves. To describe a person as, say, irritable, temperamental, easily offended is meaningful—to some extent. But the meaningfulness of that description will vary greatly depend-

ing on whether the person is sitting alone watching a sunset
or waiting for a table in a crowded restaurant. Or, in more
extreme terms, in the middle of a war or a revolution, a brave
man, or a coward, is not the same brave man, or coward, that
he is in peace time raising his family, working, etc. *Where*
one is is a very real part of *what* one is.

Here is a fairly representative example of a "where" that
is not overtly stated, but is clearly implied.

USA

X marks the spot where the body lies in time,
Bloody blotch that fell through the howling air:

By love betrayed, the letter read and burned?
Darling, I'm sorry, can't we just be friends?
By grim phone call at night, the stranger's voice
Muffled through cloth, but harder than a fist?
By dark disease, hidden from family,
But x-rays absolute proof: look, that gray blur—
With antiseptic shrug and surgical smile—
Six months, maybe a year?
                    Is there a note,
Scrawled like a scream on paper?
                        I tried, I tried!
I thought it would work. Only myself to blame.
Best years of my life. I still can't figure out
Where it went wrong. Good-bye.
                    Or a woman's name
Dropped on the pale page like dripping sound,
That one word loud as if it were live blood.

Or an address hinting it would tell all,
That proved to be his lodge, happy to send a wreath,
A bench of brothers to mourn.
                    Or a paragraph
Neat as an order book, thought out for days,
A model to be used by the next man
Tagged for that territory, giving the car,
His guns and tackle, to his oldest boy,

And all insurance to his wife (he'd been
Well-covered, naturally).
                                    Or not one word,
Just silence leering from an empty room
To hint that after liquor, drugs, and girls
He'd given up and let the lesion take him—
Guilt like an old wound groaning with the weather.
Nothing to show the weasel, conscience, snarled
Once before he grabbed it, cage and all,
And jumped into the glittering cage of air?
Nothing: no next room salesman to report
He'd heard a yell, as if one heard the blind
Cyclops bellow into his astonished cave.

But look—the cops are calling. Give 'im air.
Let the poor bastard breathe. He's coming to.

He's tougher than we thought—some broken bones,
Not much for a fall like that, he'll soon be back
Good as ever, one of the boys, to bounce
History on his knee like a bold blonde.
                                        —*Paul Engle*

The speaker here is observing a scene, in which he takes no
active part, that clearly suggests a city. No one city. But a
city, and probably a large one. This fact is important because
it sheds light on the speaker himself. He is aware of and sensitive to the impersonal, machine-like pressures of urban life.
Clues such as "no next room salesman" indicate a concern
with the rootless, transitory qualities of city life. But, further,
they indicate that the speaker himself is part of this life,
though detached in attitude. Observing the entire episode, the
attempted suicide, and stating the possible reasons for the
man's despair, make of this speaker a person who knows city
life, who feels its pain. Such a speaker differs as a person from
a speaker who is involved with, let us say, nature. Compare
the speaker of the following selection with the one described
above.

SNOWY HERON

What lifts the heron leaning on the air
I praise without a name. A crouch, a flare,
A long stroke through the cumulus of trees,
A shaped thought at the sky—then gone. *O rare!*
Saint Francis, being happiest on his knees,
Would have cried *Father!* Cry anything you please.

But praise. By any name or none. But praise
The white original burst that lights
The heron on his two soft kissing kites.
When saints praise heaven lit by doves and rays,
I sit by pond scums till the air recites
Its heron back. And doubt all else. But praise.

—*John Ciardi*

This speaker is in the country watching a heron rise from a pond. He sings the beauties of that moment in a very modern and sophisticated fashion, but it is, nevertheless, a song that is in many ways poetically conventional, even traditional.

Notice that this speaker more clearly describes the where, the setting, and is more actively involved in the scene than was the speaker of the previous selection. There, the personal pronoun "I" was never used in reference to the speaker. He was implied but never stated openly. Here, the speaker uses "I," meaning himself. He describes the scene and his reactions to it. This speaker, then, is more of a participant, less of a spectator than the previous one. He has little of the detachment and bleak humor (a humor similar to that of the first paragraph of the Dickens chapter) of the earlier speaker. He is more passionate. He describes the where, the scene, and describes it in terms that make clear his own attitudes and feelings. He relates the setting to us, asking us to join him in praise of the heron. In fact, he makes of the scene and his reactions to it a central element in his personal philosophy. To "doubt all else," but to "sit by pond scums till the air recites its heron back" certainly means that the speaker's feelings about the heron, about nature and beauty, are of fundamental importance to him. And equally certain is the fact that a speaker who finds this basic importance in the beauty of a heron is a different speaker than the one who might find the same basic importance in the beauty of music, or art, or a great machine.

Unlike the above examples, the following is an excerpt in which the setting is only vaguely implied by the speaker.

From THE EGOIST
Chapter V: Clara Middleton

[Sir Willoughby] looked the fittest; he justified the dictum of Science. The survival of the Patternes was assured. "I would," he said to his admirer, Mrs Mountstuart Jenkinson, "have bargained for health above everything but she has everything besides—lineage, beauty, breeding: is what they call an heiress, and is the most accomplished of her sex." With a delicate art he conveyed to the lady's understanding that Miss Middleton had been snatched from a crowd, without a breath of the crowd having offended his niceness. He did it through sarcasm at your modern young women, who run about the world nibbling and nibbled at, until they know one sex as well as the other, and are not a whit less cognizant of the market than men; pure, possibly; it is not so easy to say innocent; decidedly not our feminine ideal. Miss Middleton was different: she was the true ideal, fresh-gathered morning fruit in a basket, warranted by her bloom.

Women do not defend their younger sisters for doing what they perhaps have done—lifting a veil to be seen, and peeping at a world where innocence is as poor a guarantee as a babe's caul against shipwreck. Women of the world never think of attacking the sensual stipulation for perfect bloom, silver purity, which is redolent of the Oriental origin of the love-passion of their lords. Mrs Mountstuart congratulated Sir Willoughby on the prize he had won in the fair western-eastern.

"Let me see her," she said; and Miss Middleton was introduced and critically observed.

She had the mouth that smiles in repose. The lips met

full on the centre of the bow and thinned along to a lifting dimple; the eyelids also lifted slightly at the outer
corners and seemed, like the lip into the limpid cheek,
quickening up the temples, as with a run of light, or the
ascension indicated off a shoot of colour. Her features
were playfellows of one another, none of them pretending
to rigid correctness, nor the nose to the ordinary dignity
of governess among merry girls, despite which the nose
was of a fair design, not acutely interrogative or inviting
to gambols. Aspens imaged in water, waiting for the
breeze, would offer a susceptible lover some suggestion of
her face: a pure smooth-white face, tenderly flushed in
the cheeks, where the gentle dints were faintly intermelt-
ing even during quietness. Her eyes were brown, set well
between mild lids, often shadowed, not unwakeful. Her
hair of lighter brown, swelling above her temples on the
sweep to the knot, imposed the triangle of the fabulous
wild woodland visage from brow to mouth and chin, evi-
dently in agreement with her taste; and the triangle suited
her; but her face was not significant of a tameless wildness
or of weakness; her equable shut mouth threw its long
curve to guard the small round chin from that effect; her
eyes wavered only in humour, they were steady when
thoughtfulness was awakened; and at such seasons the
build of her winter-beechwood hair lost the touch of
nymph-like and whimsical, and strangely, by mere outline, added to her appearance of studious concentration.
Observe the hawk on stretched wings over the prey he
spies, for an idea of this change in the look of a young
lady whom Vernon Whitford could liken to the Mountain
Echo, and Mrs Mountstuart Jenkinson pronounced to be
a "dainty rogue in porcelain."

—*George Meredith*

Again, one must keep in mind the fact that statements
about excerpts from novels do not necessarily apply to the
entire works.

There is no specific reference in this selection to any particular setting. There are two major clues, however. The
speaker is observing Sir Willoughby and Mrs Mountstuart

Jenkinson as they talk, and is also observing Miss Middleton as she is introduced to Mrs Mountstuart. Both of these facts suggest a setting that is quiet, peaceful, and familiar—familiar to Sir Willoughby and Mrs Mountstuart Jenkinson. The scene might be the salon or the sitting-room of either of these persons. It might be the patio or garden outside the home of one or the other. It is necessarily a place that is known and is comfortable to both of them. Certainly it is not a location that is distracting in any way. If there were distractions, no matter whether they took the form of a beautiful sunset or a delicate piece of surgery, the speaker would be reacting to the setting itself. He is not. But he does seem to be included in the scene. He does not include himself as definitely as does the speaker of "Snowy Heron," and he does not divorce himself from the locale as clearly as the speaker of "USA."

It is, perhaps, possible to think of this speaker sitting in his own study, for example, speaking of the past and of another locale. To this writer, the feeling of the piece is that the speaker is there with the persons he describes. But whether one places him alone or with his characters, the important thing is that the nature of the setting remains the same. If the speaker is alone, he must be alone in a quiet, familiar place. Otherwise he would be unable to contemplate in the calmly penetrating way that he does. If he is with Willoughby and Mrs Mountstuart Jenkinson, the setting is still peaceful, undistracting, familiar. It may well be impossible to pin it down to any one place, but the characteristics of the place are quite clear. And, as with the where of any selection, these characteristics are important because they tell much about the speaker. He is, in this case, an observing, insightful, and somewhat contemplative person. He is not the participant that the speaker of "Snowy Heron" was, and he is not the spectator that the speaker of "USA" was. He is somewhere between the two. He sees the persons he is describing clearly, and is most aware of their strengths and weaknesses. There is a hint of amusement at several points—particularly when he contrasts Miss Middleton as she is with the Miss Middletons

seen by Willoughby, Whitford, and the formidable Mrs
Mountstuart Jenkinson (who, one cannot escape feeling, must
be in for a careful deflating at the hands of this speaker). The
amusement, the humor of this speaker carries with it a touch
of gentle cruelty.

The "when"

The where of literature, the locale or setting of a work, is of
basic dramatic value in determining the nature of the speaker.
One speaks differently from the stage of a huge auditorium
than from the head of a dining-room table. Analogously, the
speaker of a piece of literature is what he is partially because
of the place in which he speaks. Like the where, the time or
"when" of literature is dramatically important. Semanticists
have put great emphasis on the fact that statements should, in
some way, be dated if they are to be truly meaningful.[17] They
point out that "he is a thief" means one thing when the person
referred to steals now, and quite another when the person
referred to stole something, say, 14 years ago. They say that
we are behaving irrationally when we consider that "thief"
means the same thing when applied to the two persons.

From a different viewpoint, it is quite obvious that social
and cultural values and attitudes change. A person who is
"good" according to one scale of values is "bad" according to
another. And so it is with speakers. To advocate trade with
China, or sexual freedom, to describe with sympathy and
understanding a drug addict, or a mother-suffocated youngster—all these are one thing in 1966, but were something very
different in, for example, 1926. The speaker behind these
statements will differ depending on when he utters them.

To know a speaker means that one must know when he
spoke. Here is an example of a very clear-cut when:

OF CAUTION
Say, wouldst thou guard thy son,
That sorrow he may shun?

56

Begin at the beginning
And let him keep from sinning.
Wouldst guard thy house? One door
Make to it, and no more.
Wouldst guard thine orchard wall?
Be free of fruit to all.

—Francesco da Barberino
translated by D. G. Rossetti

Study of this selection will quickly disclose the pertinent
when facts. The words "thy" and "thine," and especially the
word "wouldst," indicate quite clearly that this speaker is not
speaking today. He belongs to the past, and the rather distant
past. This is not the language of the twentieth or nineteenth
or eighteenth centuries. It may belong to a time earlier than
the seventeenth century, but it goes at least that far back.

In addition to the language itself, there is the speaker's advice to make one door to the house. Most people today certainly do not make doors, and they certainly would not want
a house with a single door. (The line is, of course, symbolic
of far more than a literal door.) This, then, is another indication that this speaker is located in the past.

Even the statement about one's orchard wall points to the
past. It implies a time when the usual thing was to have an
orchard with or close to the house. The average present-day
suburbanite has probably had less personal experience with
orchards than with lunar probes.

Lastly, the syntax dates this speaker to some extent. Today
one would say "that he may shun sorrow," not "that sorrow
he may shun," and "make one door to it," not "one door
make to it."

Putting all this together, this speaker is most emphatically
not a modern. He chooses and uses words in ways that create
a time setting several centuries in the past. And that fact is of
much importance in determining what he is saying. The idea
that it is possible to shun sorrow, to avoid sinning, to make
one's house thoroughly safe is an extreme one in the context
of our own time. But set in the past, that idea acquires feasi-

bility, and along with it a simple strength and dignity. Few of us would agree that it is possible to avoid sin and sorrow now, whatever attitudes we may have toward these things. But it does seem possible to us that in the past, and perhaps in the past in which this speaker lives, one could avoid these pains.

The complicating, and sometimes seemingly contradictory factor is the difference between things as they were and things as they seem to have been. Even speakers who can be chronologically placed as clearly as this one are still viewed from the vantage point of today, of now. We can read and react only in the present, never in the past. And from today's viewpoint people and periods of the past often seem to have qualities that they may not, in fact, have possessed. It is easy, for example, to find in the speaker of these lines the person who deals with truth in an utterly straightforward and uncluttered fashion. For many of us today there is no such truth. But this speaker has answers that are simply and completely true. Whether or not a reader of the seventeenth century or earlier would have reacted in this manner—would have found these qualities in the speaker—is unimportant. It is a legitimate interpretation for today's reader.

Or, as another example, the French Revolution shines with the luster of history. It is one of the milestones of Western Civilization. The fact that the people who took part in that revolution may well have been at least partially unaware of many of the larger issues involved in no way invalidates the process by which today's reader creates a speaker of *The Tale of Two Cities*, for instance, who reflects that historical luster.

Objective time, the objective when of literature is, in other words, not wholly objective. It is a combination of the past as it actually was and the past as it seems today. Since it is impossible for the reader to view the past from any but his own chronological point of view, he must be aware that he may be distorting, accept that fact, and do his best to limit that distortion.

As a last comment on this selection, notice that this work

has been translated. It was written by Francesco da Barberino, an Italian poet who lived from 1264 to 1348, and translated by Dante Gabriele Rossetti who lived from 1828 to 1882. The speaker of the poem does not fit Rossetti's time and may not fit da Barberino's time. It is not necessary that he agree with either time period. He, the speaker, has his own chronology, just as he has his own personality or character.

Coexistent with the kind of objective chronology described above is the subjective or personal time placement of the speaker and the material. A man who is facing extreme old age, for instance, may be located more meaningfully in time than he would be by the date 1806 or 1953. As human beings, we exist in a sort of personal time dimension marked by familiar signposts—childhood, adolescence, marriage, birth, age, death—and the emotional states that accompany these events —the ecstasy and fear of a first love, the tenderness of marriage, the wonder of a new-born baby, the pain at the death of a loved one, the loneliness of old age. And the same is true for the speakers of literature. The reader's job, then, is to locate the speaker as accurately as possible in objective and in subjective time. Depending on the selection, one may be more important than the other, but neither can be ignored. Combined, they strengthen and make more dramatically significant the when of literature and the speaker that emerges from it.

Here is a speaker who makes very clear his place in subjective time:

REMEMBERING GOLDEN BELLS

Ruined and ill,—a man of two score;
    Pretty and guileless,—a girl of three.
Not a boy,—but still better than nothing:
To soothe one's feeling,—from time to time a kiss!
There came a day,—they suddenly took her from me;
Her soul's shadow wandered I know not where.
And when I remember how just at the time she died
She lisped strange sounds, beginning to learn to talk,
Then I know that the ties of flesh and blood
Only bind us to a load of grief and sorrow.

At last, by thinking of the time before she was born,
By thought and reason I drove the pain away.
Since my heart forgot her, many days have passed
And three times winter has changed to spring.
This morning, for a little, the old grief came back,
Because, in the road, I met her foster-nurse.
                    —Po Chü-i
                    translated by Arthur Waley

He is a forty-three-year-old man who has been reminded of
the pain his daughter's death caused. This kind of emotional
chronology may be more important, and more revealing,
than the fact that the speaker and his pain existed many centuries ago—a fact that might be guessed from certain clues in
the selection. Certainly the combination of the subjective and
objective time placement of this speaker is far more important
than either would be singly. Objectively, this speaker was a
member of a culture far different from ours. Notice the various clues that point to that fact—a girl who is better than
nothing, even though she isn't a boy—a soul's shadow—a
heart forgetting—three winters changing to spring. None of
these statements would be made by a present-day American.
But most important of all is the extreme restraint, the refine-
ment and re-refinement of feeling that this speaker expresses.
It all fits the China of centuries ago. Or rather, it fits the
modern reader's idea of the China of centuries ago. And combined with the fact that the speaker is, subjectively, no longer
young and is grieving for the little girl who died, the time
picture is quite complete. Two score is not an advanced age
today, but this speaker is a "ruined and ill" two score. In
other words, forty was older for him than it is for us. And he
is grieving. Putting it all together, this speaker exists in a
society that demands understatement, not overt expression,
and within that framework he is expressing the pain that a
personal tragedy has brought. He cannot cry out or weep,
but must state quietly and most simply a feeling that would
seem to require the strongest sort of release. All this, and
more, results from the when of this material.

As a final example of the when of a piece of literature, here is an essay whose speaker is fairly difficult to locate in time:

OF MARRIAGE AND SINGLE LIFE

He that hath wife and children hath given hostages to fortune; for they are impediments to great enterprises, either of virtue or mischief. Certainly the best works, and of greatest merit for the public, have proceeded from the unmarried or childless men, which, both in affection and means, have married and endowed the public. Yet it were great reason that those that have children should have greatest care of future times, unto which they know they must transmit their dearest pledges. Some there are who, though they lead a single life, yet their thoughts do end with themselves, and account future times impertinences; nay, there are some other that account wife and children but as bills of charges; nay, more, there are some foolish, rich, covetous men that take a pride in having no children because they may be thought so much the richer; for, perhaps they have heard some talk. *Such an one is a great rich man*, and another except to it, *Yea, but he hath a great charge of children*; as if it were an abatement to his riches. But the most ordinary cause of a single life is liberty, especially in certain self-pleasing and humorous minds, which are so sensible of every restraint as they will go near to think their girdles and garters to be bonds and shackles. Unmarried men are best friends, best masters, best servants; but not always best subjects, for they are light to run away, and almost all fugitives are of that condition. A single life doth well with churchmen, for charity will hardly water the ground where it must first fill a pool. It is indifferent for judges and magistrates; for if they be facile and corrupt, you shall have a servant five times worse than a wife. For soldiers, I find the generals commonly in their hortatives put men in mind of their wives and children; and I think the despising of marriage amongst the Turks maketh the vulgar soldier more base. Certainly wife and children are a kind of discipline of humanity; and single men, though they be many times more charitable, because their means are less exhaust, yet, on the other side, they are more cruel and hard-hearted (good to make severe inquisitors), because their tenderness is not so oft called upon. Grave natures, led by custom and therefore constant, are commonly loving husbands, as was said of Ulysses. *He preferred his aged wife Penelope to immortality.* Chaste women are often proud and forward, as presuming upon the merit of their chastity. It is one of the best bonds, both of chastity and obedience, in the wife, if she think her husband wise, which she will never do if she find him jealous. Wives are young men's mistresses, companions for middle age, and old men's nurses, so as a man may have a quarrel to marry when he will; but yet he was reputed one of the wise men that made answer to the question when a man should marry, *A young man not yet, an older man not at all.* It is often seen that bad husbands have very good wives, whether it be that it raiseth the price of their husbands' kindness when it comes, or that the wives take a pride in their patience; but this never fails, if the bad husbands were of their own choosing, against their friends' consent, for then they will be sure to make good their own folly.

—*Francis Bacon*

Where is this speaker in time? Probably most obvious is the fact that he is not speaking today. He is not a modern. The use of language makes that clear. "Hath," "yea," "maketh," "raiseth," etc., are words that modern speakers do not use. Also, the word arrangement dates this speaker, at least within broad limits.

In subjective time, too, this speaker can be placed only approximately. He is not, for example, a youngster. These are not the statements of a particularly young man. He is "mature," whatever that means. By today's standards, it probably means somewhere between thirty and sixty. To this writer's ear, the speaker of this piece would seem to be in his forties or fifties.

Here, then, is a speaker from the past, at least 200 years

into the past, perhaps more, who is/was not a youth but of a certain age. These two kinds of dating say much about the speaker and about the reader's job of discovering and relating to him. For instance, he is, by our standards, extremely formal and ornate in his use of language. And he is an absolutist— he makes flat statements, rarely qualifying them. These qualities would seem out of place today, but in this speaker's time, they were not out of place. One could make broad, sweeping generalizations in those days without appearing foolish. Realizing that fact, the reader can find a certain dignity and strength in this material. Clearly, the social values and attitudes of this speaker's time differ greatly from our own. And because of that difference, one can regard marriage and single life as partially unknown phenomena, when, in fact, the aspects of these kinds of life treated here are probably well known today. Notice, however, that viewed from the present time, a note of humor can easily creep into the picture. Many of these statements are so extreme that, to a modern, they are amusing. It may be impossible to avoid this element of humor, but if it is, there is no harm done. Combined with the dignity and strength mentioned above, the speaker simply becomes a bit softer and gentler. And it all happens as a result of the when of the piece.

Summary

Time and place are aspects of the speaker that must be discovered by the reader. Until speakers are located, are rooted in these two dimensions, they are at best, incomplete, at worst, meaningless figures. The reader functions at a given point in time and space, and his creation, the speaker, must do the same.

CHAPTER FOUR

The "how" of literature

❦

THE "HOW" of literature is a factor considerably more complex than the two dramatic elements discussed in the preceding chapter, and also, unlike them, is not found in a clearer or more specific form in writing for the theatre. Some writers have used the question "how?" to refer to the emotional tone the speaker uses. For example, how does the speaker say a particular thing—angrily, sadly, lovingly, searingly? It is this writer's belief, however, that, in that sense, "how" it is said is an integral part of what is said. The anger or fear or rapture in the speaker's words is a basic and inseparable part of the meaning of those words.

This text, therefore, will use the question "how?" to mean the combination of literary form and function that the speaker uses. There are some basic questions that must be answered here: What are the most fundamental categories of literature in terms of form? In terms of function? In functional or operational terms, what do words such as "poetry," "prose," "verse," etc., mean?[18] What is "poetic prose"?

Traditionally, prose and poetry have been used as opposites. This writer knows of no *operational* definitions of these terms as they are conventionally used. But poetry seems to mean something like "expressive or beautiful or imaginative language that has a rhythmic structure." And prose seems to mean "ordinary or everyday language that does not have a rhythmic structure." The various dictionary definitions go about like that.

Problems arise immediately. If poetry is "expressive or beautiful or imaginative language that has a rhythmic structure," what shall we call expressive or beautiful or imaginative language that does *not* have a rhythmic structure? Or, if prose is "ordinary, everyday language that does not have a rhythmic structure," what shall we call ordinary, everyday language that *does* have a rhythmic structure? There seem to be two factors involved here—expressive or beautiful language versus ordinary, i.e., not especially expressive, language, and rhythm versus lack of rhythm. But the conventional definitions do not take both factors into account. They attempt to combine them into a single element, and in so doing make definitions that are not workable.

When one adds the term verse, the complications multiply. As it is ordinarily used, verse means something like "language that has a clearly defined rhythmic structure," *or* "poetry that is based on a rhythmic structure," *or* "the language of poetry." All three are common dictionary definitions. But if verse is "language that has a clearly defined rhythmic structure," then it is the rhythmic opposite of prose, and that seems to create a category in between prose and poetry. If verse is "poetry that is based on a rhythmic structure," what shall we call poetry that is *not* based on a rhythmic structure, since, apparently, there is poetry that is not verse? If verse is "the language of poetry," the two seem to be synonyms.

Verse and prose

The problems that arise from the conventional use of these terms seem to this writer impossible to solve. Therefore, in this book, an approach will be taken that has been implied or partially stated by writers dating from Aristotle, but that has, oddly enough, rarely been openly and completely discussed.[19] That approach is as follows: there are four categories that are basic to all literature. Two of them have to do with form, two with function. Beginning with the two that relate to form, any piece of literature is, in terms of form, either *verse* or *prose*. These two, verse and prose, are opposites. And although there are many formalistic devices that are used by writers of each of these literary forms, there is one that is of primary importance. That one is *rhythm. Verse is language characterized by a sustained and perceptible rhythm. Prose is language characterized by the absence of a sustained and perceptible rhythm.* Rhythm is a complicated thing, and there are many differences in the rhythmic patterns that occur in literature. All these patterns, however, involve the time dimension, and that fact is of basic importance in any concept of rhythm. Rhythm necessarily involves time. To be rhythmic, the thing must begin at some point in time, grow, repeat itself, etc. Without the time dimension, the term rhythm is meaningless, except in the sense that some pattern is involved. A pattern, a visual pattern, is involved in the design of wallpaper, or the keys of a typewriter, but these things are certainly not rhythmic in the same way that a dancer's motions or musical selections are rhythmic. Rhythm is time based, and the time element must be kept in mind, especially where language is concerned. Written language does not involve time. A printed page exists at a given point in time, and exists in its entirety at that point. In other words, a printed page is like the wallpaper and the typewriter keys—the time dimension is not included, and, therefore, there is no rhythm. Only when language is lifted off the page and turned into silent or audible speech is it possible for rhythm to exist.

Written language is never rhythmic. Oral language may be rhythmic. If it is, repetition must occur. In addition to the element of time, rhythm requires that something be repeated, and that that something be repeated at similar time intervals. The phenomenon that is repeated need not recur in precisely the same form, but it must be recognizable. Also, the repetitions need not occur in every elapsed time interval. The commonplace drumbeat that goes *boom* (pause), *boom* (pause), *boom, boom, boom* is proof of this fact. A pause follows each of the first beats, but in marking time, or in tapping a foot, those pauses are included in the rhythm, a rhythm that goes One, two, One, two, One, two, One, two. The first, second, and fourth "two's" are not indicated by drumbeats, but we feel them as part of the rhythm nonetheless. (Exactly the same thing happens with the sort of rhythmic language that is called trimeter.)

Putting all this together, rhythm can be defined as *the awareness of and response to the passage of perceptibly similar time intervals, some or all of which are marked by the repetition of some phenomenon.*

In verse, one of two phenomena is repeated. In metrical verse, the foot (a combination of one stressed syllable and one or more unstressed syllables) is repeated; in free verse, the phrase (a group of words tied together by meaning) is repeated.[20] It is possible to have other rhythms based on the repetition of other phenomena, so long as the repetitions occur at similar time intervals, but the two described above are the ones that are most frequently used.

For example, this is verse:

> Thirty days hath September,
> April, June, and November,
> etc.,

And this:

> *From* NO PLATONIC LOVE
> Tell me no more of minds embracing minds,
>   And hearts exchang'd for hearts;
> That spirits spirits meet, as winds do winds,
>   And mix their subt'lest parts;
> That two unbodied essences may kiss,
> And then like angels, twist and feel one Bliss.
> I was that silly thing that once was wrought
>   To practise this thin love;
> I climb'd from sex to soul, from soul to thought;
>   But thinking there to move,
> Headlong I rolled from thought to soul, and then
> From soul I lighted at the sex again.
>   —*William Cartwright*

And this:

> There was an old man of Boulogne
> Who sang a most topical song.
>   It wasn't the words
>   Which frightened the birds,
> But the horrible double entendre.
>   —*Anonymous*

And this:

> *From* POUR US WINE
> By herself she is fearless
> And gives her arms to the air,
> The limbs of a long camel that has not borne.
> She gives the air her breasts,
> Unfingered ivory.
> She gives the air her long self and her curved self,
> And hips so round and heavy that they are tired.
> All these noble abundances of girlhood
> Make the doors divinely narrow and myself insane.
> Columns of marble and ivory in the old way,
> And anklets chinking in gold and musical bracelets.
> Without her I am a she-camel that has lost,
> And howls in the sand at night.
> Without her I am as sad as an old mother
> Hearing of the death of her many sons.
>   —*Ibn Kolthúm*
>   *translated by E. Powys Mathers*

And this:

> I KNEW A WOMAN LOVELY IN HER BONES
> I knew a woman, lovely in her bones,
> When small birds sighed, she would sigh back at them;
> Ah, when she moved, she moved more ways than one:
> The shapes a bright container can contain!
> Of her choice virtues only gods should speak,
> Or English poets who grew up on Greek
> (I'd have them sing in chorus, cheek to cheek.)

How well her wishes went! She stroked my chin,
She taught me Turn, and Counter-turn, and Stand;
She taught me Touch, that undulant white skin:
I nibbled meekly from her proffered hand;
She was the sickle; I, poor I, the rake,
Coming behind her for her pretty sake
(But what prodigious mowing we did make.)

Love likes a gander, and adores a goose:
Her full lips pursed, the errant note to seize;
She played it quick, she played it light and loose;
My eyes, they dazzled at her flowing knees;
Her several parts could keep a pure repose,
Or one hip quiver with a mobile nose
(She moved in circles, and those circles moved.)

Let seed be grass, and grass turn into hay:
I'm martyr to a motion not my own;
What's freedom for? To know eternity.
I swear she cast a shadow white as stone.
But who would count eternity in days?
These old bones live to learn her wanton ways:
(I measure time by how a body sways.)

—Theodore Roethke

All these are verse. In each of them there is a "sustained and perceptible rhythm." Further, in all but one of the selections, that rhythm can be clearly and specifically quantified in terms of syllables, i.e., it is metrical rhythm. But while they are all verse in terms of form, they are certainly unlike in function. It would be difficult indeed to maintain that "Thirty days hath September" and the limerick have the same emotional effect on readers that the other three pieces do, or that the other three are of equal power and worth. These selections, then, have a common form, but widely differing functions. They are all verse in form, but the term verse refers solely to the rhythmic structure of the piece. It does not indicate that the material is or is not poetry.

Here is the other side of the coin. This is prose:

From EXPLORATION BY AIR, PART II

For we are talking about a kind of existence, the newly tenanted sky, the bird's aspect of the world to which you have by now grown used. To the groundling the sky is a venture above him always prohibited, and the wind is a force and a motion; he sees it over the airport as the straightening windsock, as a shower of leaves, as spiralling dust. But for you the wind is your step, is your stairway; and you gun the engine and streak forward into it, and with a single giant stride you are in it, climbing: the wind is a place you inhabit.

—Fleming MacLeish

And this:

From THE COMIC SPIRIT

. . . It [the comic spirit] has the sage's brows, and the sunny malice of a faun lurks at the corners of the half-closed lips drawn in an idle wariness of half-tension. That slim feasting smile, shaped like the long-bow, was once a big round Satyr's laugh, that flung up the brows like a fortress lifted by gunpowder. The laugh will come again, but it will be of the order of the smile, finely-tempered, showing sunlight of the mind, mental richness, rather than noisy enormity . . .

—George Meredith

And this:

From THE DEVIL AND DANIEL WEBSTER

. . . The chickens he raised were all white meat down through the drumsticks, the cows were tended like children, and the big ram he called Goliath had horns with a curl like a morning-glory vine and could butt through an iron door. But Dan'l wasn't one of your gentlemen farmers; he knew all the ways of the land, and he'd be up by candle-light to see that the chores got done. A man with a mouth like a mastiff, a brow like a mountain, and eyes like burning anthracite—that was Dan'l Webster in his prime.

—*Stephen Vincent Benét*

And this:

As with the first group of selections, all of these have the same basic form, i.e., are prose. Also like the first group, they differ widely in function. They are all prose, but prose means that there is no "sustained and perceptible rhythm" present. It does not mean that the thing is or is not poetry. The examples of prose given above will probably cause few objections. And that is because most of us are eye-minded. If it looks like prose, if the lines run margin to margin, it *is* prose, we say. But prose is a form that depends on a rhythmic factor, and the visual line has no *necessary* rhythmic value. For instance, these sentences could be put into lines of arbitrary length as follows:

> But prose is a form
> that depends on a rhythmic factor,
> and the visual line has no *necessary*
> rhythmic value.
> For instance,
> this very paragraph
> could be put into lines of arbitrary length
> as follows.

And this certainly would not turn it from prose to verse. To take such a point of view would be to leave prose and verse to the mercies of the typographer. And since the above example does not become verse because of a visual arrangement, or rearrangement, it follows that other examples are not verse simply because of the patterns they create on the printed page. This, for instance, *is* verse:

From ANNABEL LEE

It was many and many a year ago,
　In a kingdom by the sea,
That a maiden there lived whom you may know
　By the name of Annabel Lee;—
And this maiden she lived with no other thought
　Than to love and be loved by me.

—Edgar Allan Poe

But this is not:

PART OF PLENTY

When she carries food to the table and stoops down
—Doing this out of love—and lays soup with its good
Tickling smell, or fry winking from the fire
And I look up, perhaps from a book I am reading
Or other work: there is an importance of beauty
Which can't be accounted for by there and then,
And attacks me, but not separately from the welcome
Of the food, or the grace of her arms.

When she puts a sheaf of tulips in a jug
And pours in water and presses to one side
The upright stems and leaves that you hear creak,
Or loosens them, or holds them up to show me,
So that I see the tangle of their necks and cups
With the curls of her hair, and the body they are held
Against, and the stalk of the small waist rising
And flowering in the shape of breasts;

Whether in the bringing of the flowers or the food
She offers plenty, and is part of plenty,
And whether I see her stooping, or leaning with the
　flowers,
What she does is ages old, and she is not simply,
No, but lovely in that way.

—Bernard Spencer

Both appear on the page in lines of arbitrary length. But if one were to hear "Annabel Lee" read aloud one would be quite aware of a rhythmic pattern, while if one heard "Part of Plenty" read aloud there would be no "sustained, perceptible rhythm." Rhythm must include the time dimension. Printed pages do not. They are spatial phenomena. Language, then, must be lifted off the printed page and "translated" into the time dimension (either in the form of silent reading which we hear in our minds' ears, or in the form of reading aloud which is heard by both reader and audience) in order to become rhythmic. The art of versification is steeped in visually-based definitions and attitudes, and separating the supposed from the actual rhythmic forms involved is difficult.

Poetry and nonpoetry

The first group of selections presented above is verse, the second group is prose. The two groups can be clearly and meaningfully separated on the basis of the presence or absence of rhythm. Obviously, however, the selections within each group differ. No one would say that "Thirty days hath September" or the limerick is the same sort of writing as "No Platonic Love," or "Pour Us Wine," or "I Knew a Woman, Lovely in Her Bones." No one would say that the paragraph of which this sentence is a part and the advertisement labelled "Special Purchase" is the same sort of writing as "Exploration by Air," or "The Comic Spirit," or "The Devil and Daniel Webster." We say these works are different because they affect us differently.

What, then, is the factor that makes for this difference? It is the effect that language has on its readers or hearers *and* the means used to achieve that effect. The effect can be described simply enough as an "emotionally pleasurable response." "Emotionally," meaning not intellectually, assuming the two can be separated. And "pleasurable" meaning satisfying in some way, not merely a response of giddy giggles. We respond in this "emotionally pleasurable" way to many things in literature—to the plot of a play or novel, to the characters in a short story, etc. And at times we respond in this same way to a basic function of language. Consider the last few lines from "I Knew a Woman, Lovely in Her Bones":

> I'm a martyr to a motion not my own:
> What's freedom for? To know eternity.
> I swear she cast a shadow white as stone.
> But who would count eternity in days?
> These old bones live to learn her wanton ways:
> (I measure time by how a body sways.)

One of the things that stands out in this short excerpt is the third line, and particularly "cast a shadow white as stone." This is not a literally true statement. Shadows are not white, and stones are not often white. What does it mean, then? If it is meaningful, but is literally untrue, it must be metaphor, as described in Chapter Two. To cast such a shadow would mean something like the fact that the woman was so dazzlingly, brilliantly beautiful that her radiance illuminated even her shadow. And yet her beauty was so real, so palpable, that even her shadow become concrete (no pun intended). Further, the reality of her shadow was like the purity of white stone, perhaps marble. Some meaning of this sort is involved in that one line.

Are there other metaphors in the excerpt? "Martyr to a motion not my own" is one. There is no literal martyrdom to motion. "These old bones live to learn her wanton ways" is another. Bones don't live, actually, and they certainly don't learn.

Is there symbolism here, too? "But who would count eternity in days" means, symbolically, who would try to measure perfection in small, common terms. "I measure time by how a body sways" means, symbolically, it is her motion, not the sun's, that marks my hours, and, therefore, she is my sun, the symbolic center of my universe.

This excerpt, then, is replete with metaphor and symbolism. Now consider these lines from "The Comic Spirit":

> That slim feasting smile, shaped like the long-bow, was once a big round Satyr's laugh, that flung up the brows like a fortress lifted by gunpowder.

A smile is not slim and it does not feast. Neither is it literally shaped like a long-bow. A laugh, no matter how big, does not literally fling up the brows, and that movement of the brows is not literally like a fortress lifted by gunpowder. Again, the excerpt is full of metaphor. The two differ in form: "I Knew a Woman, Lovely in Her Bones" is verse, "The Comic Spirit" is prose. But they both use metaphor and/or symbolism to achieve their effects. In other words, *both are poetry*. They are different in form, but alike in function.

For the other side of the picture, "Thirty days hath September/April, June, and November" does not involve metaphor or symbolism. It is an example of literally true language operating in a straightforward fashion. The advertisement, also, is an example of language that does not depend on metaphor or symbolism. In other words, *neither is poetry*. "Thirty days hath September" is verse, the advertisement is prose. They are different in form, but alike in function.

Putting all this together, poetry can be defined as *language which, by its use of metaphor and/or symbolism, creates an emotionally pleasurable response*. Applying the definition to the examples given above, "Thirty days hath September" and the limerick are verse but are *not* poetry. The excerpts from "No Platonic Love" and "Pour Us Wine," and the selection "I Knew a Woman, Lovely in Her Bones" are *both* verse *and* poetry. The excerpts from "Exploration by Air," "The Comic Spirit," and "The Devil and Daniel Webster" are *both* prose *and* poetry. The advertisement is prose but is *not* poetry. Those selections that are poetry, whether prose or verse, create an "emotionally pleasurable response" *by* using metaphor and/or symbolism.

The following schematic device may help:

The above circle represents all of literature.[21] There are four basic categories, two that pertain to form, two to function. Since there is no word in the language that means the opposite of poetry, the synthetic term "nonpoetry" is used to complete the picture. Nonpoetry, of course, is language which does not create an emotionally pleasurable response by its use of metaphor and/or symbolism. In literature, as in other areas, it is impossible to have a form that is without function or a function that is formless. Therefore, two of the above terms are needed to accurately label a piece of literature. It is *verse-poetry*, *prose-poetry*, *verse-nonpoetry*, or *prose-nonpoetry*. Any and every piece of literature will fall into one of these categories.

Notice some of the advantages of the above approach. It is no longer necessary to call both a dirty limerick and a Shakespearean sonnet poetry—and if one equates verse and poetry, that is a necessity. And the uncomfortable vagueness of the term "poetic prose," whatever it means, can now be avoided. But most important of all, these are operational definitions. Of the scores of definitions of poetry, prose, and verse, few, if any, have been functional. Some of them are, themselves, poetry—for instance, "poetry is man's most silent song." But with the definitions suggested above, it is possible to operationally identify and meaningfully label literature.

Speakers of verse-poetry, verse-nonpoetry, prose-poetry, and prose-nonpoetry

Now, what has this whole business to do with the speakers of literature? How does a speaker differ depending on whether he speaks in verse-poetry, verse-nonpoetry, prose-poetry, or prose-nonpoetry? First of all, verse has to do with form, and it may have to do with a very specific and demanding form if it is metrical verse. A speaker who chooses verse form is choosing to speak, to operate, within a particular artistic discipline. In addition to expressing his ideas and feelings, he must express them within a given framework. Suppose, for instance, he wishes to communicate the idea that the twin burden of consciousness and mortality is an impossible one for a human being to bear. (For the moment the issue of whether he will speak in poetry or nonpoetry is being ignored.) To state that idea is one thing, but to state it within the framework of, say, trochaic tetrameter is quite another. The trochaic foot consists of one stressed and one unstressed syllable, and tetrameter consists of four beats to the rhythmic phrase. "The twin burden of consciousness and mortality is an impossible one for a human being to bear" must then be put into words that have the rhythmic pattern DUM-da-DUM-da-DUM-da-DUM-da. And the statement must be worded in such a way as to fit the required rhythmic pattern without damaging the meaning by seeming wooden or artificial or mechanical. If it is done well, it will seem to the reader that the rhythmic form fits the meaning perfectly, that the author has found the only completely right way to say what he said.

A speaker who chooses such a form is deliberately imposing restrictions upon himself. He is deliberately assuming the responsibility of meeting the demands of the verse form. Basically, he is doing this because he feels that to work within the particular form is to enrich, to make more significant his statement. Robert Frost said, "Freedom is feeling easy in your harness."[22] T. S. Eliot put it, "Freedom is only true freedom when it appears against the background of an artificial limitation."[23] Speakers who choose verse forms, then, are not seeking some sort of unlimited or complete freedom of expression. They feel that such freedom is meaningless. The freedom they desire is the sort that rests on a thorough mastery of form—the freedom that demands that artistic techniques be so skillfully used that they are unobtrusive, or, at best, unnoticeable.

Such speakers might be called artistically mature. Certainly they must be acquainted with many kinds of form. And they clearly work in a manner that involves restraint and control. They are literary sophisticates. Lastly, they have a kind of courage. When they fail they may well fail hugely. If form and function are not well-matched, if the artistic techniques are too apparent, their statements may degenerate into sing-songy doggerel. (The writers of claptrap verse are not being considered here. It is the serious, the gifted verse-maker who may fail dismally.)

Prose, of course, has a form, too. It does not have "a sustained and perceptible rhythm," but it does include grammatical, syntactical, and stylistic elements that make demands on speakers. There is more variation in the formalistic demands of prose than in those of verse. With much verse, the rhythmic demands are the same throughout the selection. In prose, the speaker will very frequently use, say, short, terse sentences in one part of the material, and long, sweeping, parallel constructions in another part. It is safe to say that the speakers of prose are meeting formalistic requirements that differ from those of verse, and it seems permissible to say that the speakers of prose are less limited, less constrained by form than the speakers of verse. If one accepts the point made by Frost and Eliot, however, this lack of limitation or restriction gives prose speakers less, not more, freedom. It apparently comes down to something like this: the speakers who choose prose operate within a more flexible artistic framework; they can concern themselves more directly with the what of the material since they are not bound by a specific rhythmic structure; they sound less formal and elaborate (and, to some ears, less forbidding) because the structure of prose is more like the structure of everyday speech.

The relationships between verse and prose and the speaker constitute half the picture. There is no such thing as verse or prose *per se*. It will be verse-poetry, verse-nonpoetry, prose-poetry, or prose-nonpoetry. Speakers who choose poetry do so because what they want to say cannot be said in nonpoetry. As has already been pointed out, poetry involves the creation of new meaning by the use of metaphor and/or symbolism. The speaker of poetry, then, is saying something that has not been said before, saying something for the first time. Since there are no known or conventional ways of saying what he wants to say, he is faced with the problem of saying it in a new way that will necessarily make for obliqueness, indirection, describing the unknown in terms of the known, etc. Such a speaker has, first of all, the awareness of this new meaning, and, second, the desire or need to express, to communicate that meaning. These two elements set him apart from the speakers of nonpoetry. It is possible to go so far as to say that poets (along with the other artists of the world) are a bit mad—that they must be in order to combine the sharply edged sensitivity that they possess with the drive, the compulsion to communicate. But without going to such an extreme, it would certainly appear that to deal emotionally with the known is simpler and safer than dealing with the unknown. Poets, then, do not choose the simple and the safe. And if that is true of the actual poets, it is far truer of the speakers of poetry. In fact, it is true of the speaker whether or not it is true of the poet.

The speakers of nonpoetry, as has already been implied, do not face the danger and the difficulty of creating new meaning. They work with the familiar, not in the sense of working with the ordinary or trite, but in the sense of working with words that, instead of being used or combined in new ways, have commonly understood meanings. They operate in more direct and straightforward ways than do the speakers of nonpoetry.

It should, perhaps, be emphasized again that the speaker of a selection has no necessary relationship with the author of that selection. Therefore, the above statements about the speakers of various kinds of material have no necessary application to the authors of those materials.

Two of the terms verse, prose, poetry, and nonpoetry are

THE "HOW" OF LITERATURE

needed to label a selection. Thus, one will be dealing with the speakers, not of verse, prose, poetry, and nonpoetry, but of verse-poetry, verse-nonpoetry, prose-poetry, and prose-nonpoetry. Before commenting on these speakers, however, there is one further point to be made. The four categories listed above are basic. Any and every piece of literature is verse-poetry, verse-nonpoetry, prose-poetry, or prose-nonpoetry. These categories are fundamental, but they are not the only ones that exist. In addition to being, say, prose-nonpoetry, a given selection may be a short story; in addition to being verse-poetry, a work may be a play. These further or secondary forms bring dimensions and demands of their own. They bring other characteristics to the speakers involved. It is interesting to note, though, that the vast majority of the verse-poetry of the world is just that—verse-poetry. It does not fall into other categories. The same is true of verse-nonpoetry. Most of it belongs to no other type or category of literature. But with prose-poetry, though much of it is simply that, a great deal of it is, in addition, in the form of a play, a short story, an essay, etc. And with prose-nonpoetry the difference is greatest of all. Most of it is, in addition to being prose-nonpoetry, something else—a play, a novel, etc.

Bearing all this in mind, it would seem that the speakers of verse-poetry are persons with a keen and often painful sensitivity, a deep need to voice the newness of their feelings, an awareness of and, perhaps, preoccupation with form, and a concern and involvement with a literary category that allows them little time or energy to deal with other formalistic requirements.

The speakers of verse-nonpoetry are also aware of form, but they are not striving for new meanings, and, apparently, this leaves them free to seek other effects—humor, satire, cajolery, etc.

The speakers of prose-poetry are committed to the new, but they are not bound to a basic form, and, therefore, they are much freer to deal with secondary forms—plays, narratives, etc.

The speakers of prose-nonpoetry are freest of all. They do not deal with the new and are not restricted by basic forms. Thus, they can concentrate more completely on stylistic matters and on the secondary forms involved.

Summary

The dramatic elements of literature are represented by the terms "who," "what," "where," "when," and "how." In a sense, the "who" of literature, the speaker, is the all-important concept. But speakers do not exist in a dramatic vacuum. They say something in some place at some time in some way. It is both meaningless and impossible to conceive of a speaker who states nothing, at no point in time or space, and in no way. And it is impossible to create a complete speaker if any one of these elements is lacking. There is an analogy of a sort between these dramatic dimensions and the four dimensional space-time continuum. Just as one cannot locate an airplane or a building or an atom without the three dimensions of space and the one of time, one cannot locate a speaker without considering what he says, where he says it, when he says it, and how he says it. To approach literature as dramatic discourse, then, requires that one relate to speakers in terms of where, when, and how they say what they have to say.

CHAPTER FIVE

"To whom"

✿

SEVERAL writers in the field of Oral Interpretation have dealt with the dramatic elements represented by the questions Who? What? Where? When? and How? Some of these writers have included another element represented by the question "to whom?"[24] Their thought is that if a piece of literature is essentially dramatic, is essentially a statement by some one, at some time, in some place, stated in some way, it must also be a statement *to someone.* The speaker, in other words, is assumed to be speaking to a particular audience of one or more people, or, at least, to a certain sort of mentality or personality.

This text will take the view that the element represented by the question "to whom?" does not exist in literature, or, at most, exists only in very bad literature. It would be simple enough to make this point, and to proceed with the rest of the book. But a very important aspect of literature is involved in the acceptance or rejection of the "to whom?" element, and that aspect requires comment.

First of all, the idea that literature is not addressed to any particular person(s) is not new or original with this writer. In *The Well-Tempered Critic*, Northrop Frye deals with the idea that a poet is one part of a whole personality, that the poetic being is separate from the ordinary being. He says that within the individual's total personality, there is a part that is poet and a part that is man, and that the two must be kept separate. He goes on,

> As soon as it is felt that a writer is showing off, that he is taking his eye away from his form and is beginning to introduce things that he cannot resist, a barrier goes up at once. The reason is that a self-conscious cleverness interrupting the unity of the form is an intervention from the ordinary personality, with its claims to attention, a kind of attempt at direct address from the author as "man." *The barrier is a sign that direct address, which has no place in literature as such, is being resisted.*[25] (Italics mine.)

In *The Sound, Sense, and Performance of Literature,* another work that should be required reading, Don Geiger discusses his own and others' views on this point. He says,

> To think that serious literature is actually "addressed" to somebody or to some particular mental and psychological limitations is, ordinarily, to commit the fallacy of confusing a piece of literature with a whisky advertisement. Even superior work which seems to "address" a particular audience—one recalls, for example, Pope's satires, the occasional poetry of Dryden, even some of the work of Shakespeare—is memorable, we think, because it was so well formed that it transcended its local purpose. Much of the worst of these—and other—writers' work is bad, we suppose, just because it was so particularly "addressed" to some particular audience. In our time, no one has been more insistent on the "communicative" aspects of literature than I. A. Richards, yet he concludes that, "Those artists and poets who can be suspected of close separate attention to the communicative aspect tend . . . to fall into a subordinate rank." Richard Wilbur writes suggestively of this matter, "A poem is addressed to the Muse," and then he says explicitly that with which most serious writers would surely agree: "During the act of writing, the poem is an effort to express a knowledge imperfectly

felt, to articulate relationships not quite seen, to make or discover some pattern in the world. It is a conflict with disorder, not a message from one person to another. Once the poem is written and published, however, it belongs to anyone who will take it, and the more the better."[26]

These two writers, of the many who have made this point directly or indirectly, are quoted here because they seem to work especially well with the point of view of this text. The first, Northrop Frye, in saying that the real man, the real author, should not come into direct contact with the audience, seems to agree with this text's view that the speaker is not a real person, and is certainly not the real author. The second, Don Geiger, in saying that literature does not function as an advertisement or a personal message, seems to agree with this text's view that literature must involve indirection in the form of imaginative or metaphorical or subjective insights. Both authors are using the term literature in the narrower or more specific sense referred to earlier.

If one combines a statement about the necessary indirectness of literature with a statement about the scope of literature, one may say that only those kinds of writing that allow for the indirectness referred to, that allow for the existence of a speaker, qualify as literature, in the more specific sense. In application, this definition makes for some interesting distinctions. For example, many speeches *as delivered orally* will not qualify as literature. They bring a real speaker into direct and purposeful contact with a real audience. But those same speeches, preserved in written form, may be literature *if* they can appeal to more than the original, specific audience. They can acquire, in other words, a speaker in the dramatic or unreal sense of that word. This idea is, of course, similar to the Aristotelian concepts of *rhetoric* and *poetic*. Rhetoric, for Aristotle, was language used in such a way as to change ideas, attitudes, or actions; poetic was language used in such a way as to bring esthetic or emotional pleasure. To change attitudes or actions ordinarily means that a real speaker must come into direct contact with an audience; to bring emotional pleasure ordinarily means that there is no contact between a real speaker and an audience, but that the unreal speaker is the necessary link, or distance, or barrier, between the reader and the literature.

The concept of the indirectness of literature, the lack of a specific audience, is important in the frame of reference of this book because only by a combination of a universal appeal (or as close to that as possible) and a speaker does literature become available to all. If it is a question of a direct statement, a direct link between a real author and a specific audience, even if that audience is specified only in terms of intellectual and emotional abilities, it becomes a "closed circuit" of sorts into which the reader will be unable to enter, unless he happens to fit into the prescribed audience group. But if it is a statement by an unreal speaker, not directed toward any specified audience, that speaker can include the reader himself. To put it differently, the literature must have room in it for the reader. He must be able to function within the literary work, and to function in a dramatic fashion.

Here, for instance, is an excerpt from a work that does not allow the reader to enter and work within in a dramatic manner:

> Structural and transactional analysis offer a systematic, consistent theory of personality and social dynamics derived from clinical experience, and an actionistic, rational form of therapy which is suitable for, easily understood by, and naturally adapted to the great majority of psychiatric patients.[27]

This material links the reader directly to the author. The obvious intent here is to inform and to convince the reader of the validity of the statements made. And these purposes are achieved by logical and intellectual means. The reader's feelings are not involved to any significant extent. Notice that the dramatic elements "who," "what," "where," "when," and "how" are practically nonexistent. The use of language is rather modern, and that might date the selection within broad limits, but there is no hint of a setting, no combination of form and function, and, therefore, no speaker. This material, then, is not literature in the narrow sense of the word. It is psychology.

By contrast, here is an excerpt from a selection that is open to the reader, that admits and involves him.

> Millions upon millions of years ago, when the continents were already formed and the principal features of the earth had been decided, there existed, then as now, one aspect of the world that dwarfed all others. It was a mighty ocean, resting uneasily to the east of the largest continent, a restless ever-changing, gigantic body of water that would later be described as pacific.
>
> Over its brooding surface immense winds swept back and forth, whipping the waters into towering waves that crashed down upon the world's seacoasts, tearing away rocks and eroding the land. In its dark bosom, strange life was beginning to form, minute at first, then gradually of a structure now lost even to memory. Upon its farthest reaches birds with enormous wings came to rest, and then flew on.
>
> Agitated by a moon stronger then than now, immense tides ripped across this tremendous ocean, keeping it in a state of torment. Since no great amounts of sand had yet been built, the waters where they reached shore were universally dark, black as night and fearful.
>
> Scores of millions of years before man had risen from the shores of the ocean to perceive its grandeur and to venture forth upon its turbulent waves, this eternal sea existed, larger than any other of the earth's features, vaster than the sister oceans combined, wild, terrifying in its immensity and imperative in its universal role.[28]

This is literature. The intent here is not to inform (although the speaker does convey some information), but to involve us, as the speaker is involved, in the wonder of growth and change and time. There is no neutral position taken by this speaker. Instead, his feelings are consistently apparent. He describes the ocean as "resting uneasily," having a "brooding surface," a "dark bosom," "fearful" waters, as being "eternal," "wild," "terrifying," and fulfilling a "universal role." These are metaphors, and if there were many more of them the selection would be poetry. As it is, the central meaning is not dependent on metaphor, but a large amount of the flavor and color of the material is. This speaker is not describing reality *per se*, but his feelings about reality. And his feelings involve and include the reader's feelings. Whereas the first excerpt from the book on psychology is an example of material presented to the reader for his rational and logical inspection and approval, the above excerpt is an example of material that quickly envelops the reader by eliciting emotional responses. Along with the speaker, the reader *feels* about the ocean, and the process of feeling means that the reader, like the speaker, is acting and reacting dramatically.

This is another way of treating the idea that worthwhile literature requires the reader to do some of the work. If the whole thing is laid out in thorough-going, objective, scientific terms, it will not belong to the realm of literature; rather, it will belong to one of the other verbal disciplines—sociology, anthropology, etc. Literature is a creative and re-creative art. To know or understand or appreciate the work, one must re-create it. And in so doing, one makes the literature part of one's self, and becomes, one's self, a part of the literature.

This process requires that the reader "internalize" some of the emotional elements of the literature. And, oddly enough, in order for this to happen, literature must deal very largely, though not entirely, with "externals." The two terms are being used here in the sense of *external* behavior, specific acts, events, objects, etc., and *internal* behavior, emotional attitudes, feelings, drives, needs, etc. On the face of it, it might seem that the literature should go straight to the point and treat the inner states of human beings, but, by and large, when this is attempted, the literature becomes didactic, preachy, inferior, or something other than literature. Instead, by a wise and imaginative choice of externals, the author gives the reader the tools with which to complete the literary job. The author may use many techniques to avoid dealing with internals. He may avoid by the use of metaphor and symbolism, i.e., making objective phenomena stand for emotional states. He may simply treat his externals openly and directly, if they are items about which most of us have similar feelings. He may create a context in which a statement that seems simple and specific acquires multiple or paradoxical or ambiguous meanings.

Here are some examples. In Edwin Arlington Robinson's "Mr. Flood's Party," the old man, alone, friendless, and accustomed to pain, drinks from his jug,

> Then, as a mother lays her sleeping child
> Down tenderly, fearing it may awake,
> He set the jug down slowly at his feet
> With trembling care, knowing that most things break;

That phrase, "knowing that most things break," is, in context, one of the master strokes of literature. But imagine how horribly wrong it would have been if the author had said something about "knowing that promises, hopes, and hearts all break." He would have been treating the internals, but it would have been disastrous. Instead, he made a simple, seemingly uncomplicated statement about things, externals, and let the reader turn it into promises, hearts, or whatever.

Or, an obvious example, a few lines from Rupert Brooke's "The Great Lover":

> These I have loved:
>   White plates and cups, clean-gleaming,
> Ringed with blue lines; and feathery, faery dust;
> Wet roofs, beneath the lamp-light; the strong crust
> Of friendly bread; and many-tasting food;
> Rainbows; and the blue bitter smoke of wood;
> And raindrops couching in cool flowers;
> And flowers themselves, that sway through sunny hours,

Dreaming of moths that drink them under the moon;
Then, the cool kindliness of sheets that soon
Smooth away trouble; and the rough male kiss
Of blankets; grainy wood; live hair that is
Shining and free; blue-massing clouds; the keen
Unpassioned beauty of a great machine;
The benison of hot water; furs to touch;
The good smell of old clothes; and other such—
The comfortable smell of friendly fingers,
Hair's fragrance, and the musty reek that lingers
About dead leaves and last year's ferns. . .

This is simply a catalog, a list of things. But in addition to the linquistic skill with which these things are treated in metaphor, they are things about which most of us feel, and feel similarly. Imagine Brooke having said, instead of "the cool kindliness of sheets, that soon/Smooth away trouble," something like, "the wonderful feeling of relaxing in a freshly made bed with clean sheets—the feeling of letting the tiredness and tension ebb away." It would have been absurd. He would have been using internals, emotional states, instead of allowing the reader to do the work of turning those externals into his (the reader's) emotional states.

Or, a final example, this line from the last act of *Romeo and Juliet*: Juliet awakens in the tomb, sees Romeo dead, and before killing herself, kisses him. She says one simple line, "*Thy lips are warm!*" Because of the context, wrapped up in those words are all sorts of unsaid things about the unbelievability of death, the terrible immediacy of Romeo's dying, and a half-incoherent wish-belief that if his lips are warm then there is, there must be, life; these things are unsaid, because to say them would ruin the line and the entire scene. It would be an attempt at treating internals, but, as always, it would fail.

Summary

Literature is a process that involves the imaginations of an author and of many readers. It is an emotional chain that links the readers to the author, but links them loosely. One of the intermediate links in the chain is the speaker, the unreal person, the creation of the reader, and, perhaps, the poetic or imaginative part of the author. If an attempt is made to tie the reader(s) directly to the author, or vice versa, the literature fails. If the reader is allowed to work his way along the chain to the middle link, the middle man, the speaker, and then to retrace his steps to the imaginative part of himself, the literature succeeds.

CHAPTER SIX

Four sample analyses

LITERATURE is not a group of static, impersonal things. It is a series of statements, each of which involves an imaginary person, a speaker, whose character or personality fits the statement made. The reader discovers and creates the speaker by reacting to, and becoming part of what is said, in a particular setting, at a certain time, and in a given way.

In an attempt to tie together what has been said so far, and to illustrate the approach discussed, here are four sample analyses, one of verse-nonpoetry, one of prose-nonpoetry, one of verse-poetry, and one of prose-poetry.

Verse-nonpoetry

THE UNKNOWN CITIZEN

(*To* JS/07/M/378—*This Marble Monument is Erected by the State*)

He was found by the Bureau of Statistics to be
One against whom there was no official complaint,
And all the reports on his conduct agree
That, in the modern sense of an old-fashioned word,
    he was a saint,
For in everything he did he served the Greater Com-
    munity.
Except for the War till the day he retired

He worked in a factory and never got fired,
But satisfied his employers, Fudge Motors Inc.
Yet he wasn't a scab or odd in his views,
For his Union reports that he paid his dues,
(Our report on his Union shows it was sound)
And our Social Psychology workers found
That he was popular with his mates and liked a drink.
The press are convinced that he bought a paper every day
And that his reactions to advertisements were normal
   in every way.
Policies taken out in his name prove that he was fully
   insured,
And his Health-card shows that he was once in hospital
   but left it cured.
Both Producers Research and High-Grade Living declare
He was fully sensible to the advantages of the Installment
   Plan
And had everything necessary to the Modern Man,
A phonograph, a radio, a car and a frigidaire.
Our researchers into Public Opinion are content
That he held the proper opinions for the time of year;
When there was peace, he was for peace; when there was
   war, he went.
He was married and added five children to the population,
Which our Eugenist says was the right number for a
   parent of his generation,
And our teachers report that he never interfered with
   their education.
Was he free? Was he happy? The question is absurd:
Had anything been wrong, we should certainly have
   heard.

                                        —*W. H. Auden*

This selection is about a man who is dead. He is, first of all,
nameless. Instead, he has a number. Immediately, then, there
is an impersonal and chilling element involved here. The first
three lines seem quite serious and straightforward. But in the
fourth line there is an important clue to the basic nature of the
selection. The man is referred to as "a saint." The combina-

tion of "saint" and namelessness indicates rather clearly that this is satire. And from the fourth line on, the satire becomes heavier and heavier. The man is described as a complete puppet, pulled and manipulated by all sorts of forces. Even his feelings about war and peace were suitable, i.e., like those of everyone else. At the end, the issues of freedom and happiness are described as meaningless, having no place in such a world.

Since the selection is satirical, the speaker is actually saying just about the opposite of what the words mean on the surface, and he is using satire as a means of avoiding internals. The man described was not free, was not happy, and all the elements of the society that controlled him are vicious and distorting ones. The man was a slave, probed and prodded by researchers and pressure groups. He didn't even rebel against the total conformity that surrounded him. He conformed in the most dismal and deadly fashion. But the speaker does not deal explicitly with this deadly conformity. He lets the reader do that for himself.

There are few, if any, words that are at all difficult in terms of meaning. There are practically no ambiguous or multiple or paradoxical meanings involved. There is no metaphorical language or symbolism used. Thus, the selection is nonpoetry. But there is a distinct rhythmic pattern involved. It is reminiscent of the rhythm of Ogden Nash's verse—the lines of varying lengths, but marked off by a rhyme scheme. It is, then, verse-nonpoetry.

The setting, the where of the piece, is exceedingly vague. The speaker is probably in or near a large city. He is observing facets of life that are most clearly evident in urban areas. But it is hard to be more specific than that.

The when is also vague, but far less so. The speaker is not speaking from the vantage point of the nineteenth century or earlier. In fact, he very probably can be placed somewhere within the last twenty years (i.e., after 1945). The things he is observing have certainly existed for longer than that, but it is only within the last two decades that the problems of conformity within societies have become as extreme as they are pictured here. Even his terminology, "Social Psychology," "Producers Research," etc., suggests the postwar period.

There is no indication of any particular audience. The selection is there for anyone who will to approach and appropriate.

What sort of person is he, then, this speaker? He is a man of our times who is aware of and concerned about the society in which he lives. He is protesting against the manipulative and impersonal elements of his culture. His protest is not savage or slashing. It is controlled. And this control is mirrored, perhaps, in the use of a form (verse) that requires further control. He does not point out the way to change, to freedom and happiness. Indeed, he does not even indicate hope for the future. He seems to observe rather than participate. He is insightful, intelligent, but is, perhaps, emotionally armored against a too direct, too personal involvement in the pain he sees around him.

Prose-nonpoetry

Here is the second example:

> Friend and brother:—It was the will of the Great Spirit that we should meet together this day. He orders all things and has given us a fine day for our council. He has taken His garment from before the sun and caused it to shine with brightness upon us. Our eyes are opened that we see clearly; our ears are unstopped that we have been able to hear distinctly the words you have spoken. For all these favors we thank the Great Spirit, and Him only.
>
> Brother, this council fire was kindled by you. It was at your request that we came together at this time. We have listened with attention to what you have said. You requested us to speak our minds freely. This gives us great joy; for we now consider that we stand upright before you and can speak what we think. All have heard your voice and all speak to you now as one man. Our minds are agreed.

Brother, you say you want an answer to your talk before you leave this place. It is right that you should have one, as you are a great distance from home and we do not wish to detain you. But first we will look back a little and tell you what our fathers have told us and what we have heard from the white people.

Brother, listen to what we say. There was a time when our forefathers owned this great island. Their seats extended from the rising to the setting sun. The Great Spirit had made it for the use of Indians. He had created the buffalo, the deer and other animals for food. He had made the bear and the beaver. Their skins served us for clothing. He had scattered them over the country and taught us how to take them. He had caused the earth to produce corn for bread. All this He had done for His red children because He loved them. If we had some disputes about our hunting - ground they were generally settled without the shedding of much blood.

But an evil day came upon us. Your forefathers crossed the great water and landed on this island. Their numbers were small. They found friends and not enemies. They told us they had fled from their own country for fear of wicked men and had come here to enjoy their religion. They asked for a small seat. We took pity on them, granted their request, and they sat down among us. We gave them corn and meat; they gave us poison in return.

The white people, brother, had now found our country. Tidings were carried back and more came among us. Yet we did not fear them. We took them to be friends. They called us brothers. We believed them and gave them a larger seat. At length their numbers had greatly increased. They wanted more land; they wanted our country. Our eyes were opened and our minds became uneasy. Wars took place. Indians were hired to fight against Indians, and many of our people were destroyed. They also brought strong liquor among us. It was strong and powerful, and has slain thousands.

Brother, our seats were once large and yours were small. You have now become a great people, and we have scarcely a place left to spread our blankets. You have got our country, but are not satisfied; you want to force your religion upon us.

Brother, continue to listen. You say that you are sent to instruct us how to worship the Great Spirit agreeably to His mind; and, if we do not take hold of the religion which you white people teach we shall be unhappy hereafter. You say you are right and we are lost. How do we know this to be true? We understand that your religion is written in a Book. If it was intended for us, as well as you, why has not the Great Spirit given to us, and not only to us, but why did He not give to our forefathers the knowledge of that Book, with the means of understanding it rightly. We only know what you tell us about it. How shall we know when to believe, being so often deceived by the white people?

Brother, you say there is one way to worship and serve the Great Spirit. If there is but one religion, why do you white people differ so much about it? Why are not all agreed, as you can all read the Book?

Brother, we do not understand these things. We are told that your religion was given to your forefathers and has been handed down from father to son. We also have a religion which was given to our forefathers and has been handed down to us, their children. We worship in that way. It teaches us to be thankful for all the favors we receive, to love each other, and to be united. We never quarrel about religion.

Brother, the Great Spirit has made us all, but He has made a great difference between His white and His red children. He has given us different complexions and different customs. To you He has given the arts. To these He has not opened our eyes. We know these things to be true. Since He has made so great a difference between us in other things, why may we not conclude that He has given us a different religion according to our understanding? The Great Spirit does right. He knows what is best for His children; we are satisfied.

Brother, we do not wish to destroy your religion or to take it from you. We only want to enjoy our own.

Brother, you say you have not come to get our land or

our money, but to enlighten our minds. I will now tell that I have been at your meetings and saw you collect money from the meeting. I cannot tell what this money was intended for, but suppose it was for your minister; and, if we should conform to your way of thinking, perhaps you may want some from us.

Brother, we are told that you have been preaching to the white people in this place. These people are our neighbors. We are acquainted with them. We will wait a little while and see what effect your preaching has upon them. If we find it does them good, makes them honest, and less disposed to cheat Indians, we will then consider again of what you have said.

Brother, you have now heard our answer to your talk, and this is all we have to say at present. As we are going to part, we will come and take you by the hand, and hope the Great Spirit will protect you on your journey and return you safe to your friends.

The speaker of this selection discloses himself and delineates himself quite clearly. Obviously he is an American Indian speaking to a white missionary. Obviously he is speaking during the period following the white conquest of this country, for the language used and the issues raised indicate that the speech was given some time ago, perhaps during the last century. The setting is described as a council, a ceremonial council with the ritual of a council fire. In terms of form and function, the speaker is using prose-nonpoetry, although there is a certain sort of rhythm in the repetitions of the word "Brother." The speaker is clearly an intelligent man who uses logic in a most penetrating fashion. He asks what seem to be simple, almost childlike (but not childish) questions, but questions that probe into basic fallacies and contradictions in the missionary's point of view. The speech, however, is not an angry one. There is a gentleness that pervades it. The speaker says, in effect, "You have stolen our country, destroyed our way of life, imprisoned us in small places, and now you ask us to adopt the religion that prompted, or at least allowed, you to do these things." Such a statement might well be made in rage, in frustrated fury. This speaker makes that statement with a quietness and dignity and even affection for the missionary. If one accepts an operational definition of the term "Christian," this speaker seems most Christian in his behavior.

All these things are apparent in what this speaker says. Now, this is an actual speech that was delivered by an Indian warrior named Red Jacket in 1805 at a council of chiefs of the Six Nations after a white missionary had addressed them. *As delivered*, the speech probably did not qualify as literature. For one thing, it was aimed directly at a very specific audience. There is, however, so much controlled dignity in these words that one may well wonder if the speech did not affect many people beyond the immediate audience of one, assuming that it was heard or read. In any event, for today's reader, the speech has no "to whom." It is not now delivered to the white missionary. *As delivered*, there was a real speaker saying these words—Red Jacket. Today, this material involves a speaker who may or may not correspond to Red Jacket. The speaker of these words is a man of great strength, gentleness, and simplicity. Red Jacket may or may not have possessed these qualities. He may have been, in fact, deeply angered by the plight of his fellows, but aware that an expression of that anger would only have made matters worse. He may have been depressed and resigned to the tragic state in which the Indians found themselves, but may have put on a façade of dignity suitable to the ceremonial occasion at which he spoke. There is no way for the average reader to know the real Red Jacket, to see him as he was. Rather, the reader of today must deal with the speaker of this selection, and in doing so he will view the Indian warrior at a ceremonial council in 1805 from today's vantage point. Although this may involve finding in the speaker qualities that Red Jacket did not actually have, it is valid to do so because the material permits the reader to do just that. In other words, whether or not this speech was literature when it was delivered, it is literature now. And, since it is, one must approach it, and become involved in it, as dramatic discourse.

Verse-poetry

This is the third example:

REUBEN BRIGHT

Because he was a butcher and thereby
Did earn an honest living (and did right)
I would not have you think that Reuben Bright
Was any more a brute than you or I;
For when they told him that his wife must die,
He stared at them and shook with grief and fright,
And cried like a great baby half that night,
And made the women cry to see him cry.
And after she was dead, and he had paid
The singers and the sexton and the rest,
He packed a lot of things that she had made
Most mournfully away in an old chest
Of hers, and put some chopped-up cedar boughs
In with them, and tore down the slaughter-house.
                    —*Edwin Arlington Robinson*

On the face of it, the speaker here is an observer who describes the way one human being reacted to a personal tragedy. He starts out in a rather factual manner, using almost no metaphorical or ambiguous language. There is a rhythmic pattern, however. Thus, it is verse. And it would seem to be verse-nonpoetry—until the last line. Up until that point, the speaker seems to be emotionally neutral or uncommitted. There is a hint of anger in the lines

> And after she was dead, and he had paid
> The singers and the sexton and the rest,

for having to pay for such things at such a time seems an extreme and ugly sort of commerciality. But other than those lines, the speaker seems rather unmoved.

The time is clearly not the present. It is, perhaps, the early part of this century—a time when "chopped-up cedar

boughs" and "slaughter-houses" were commonplace. The setting is either a small town or a country village, certainly not
a great city. There is no specified audience. In the third line,
the words, "I would not have you think" are not directed toward any particular "you." "You" is anyone who will listen.

And then comes the last line—the strength of the selection,
and the thing that makes it poetry. It is not metaphorical
language. The statement is literally true. Reuben Bright did
tear down the slaughterhouse. But it is symbolic language. In
addition to its literally true meaning, it operates on several
other levels. A slaughterhouse is a place of killing, of death.
Reuben Bright, sickened by his wife's death, and sickened of
death itself, wanted nothing around him to remind him of his
own loss or of death in general. But he was a butcher. And in
that time a butcher did his own killing. For anyone, doctor,
lawyer, etc., to have torn down the slaughterhouse would
have meant a deep need to push death in any form away. But
for a butcher, one who had accepted death as a commonplace
daily event, the act means a new view of himself. Reuben was
seeing himself through new eyes, and he wanted no part of
death, even though it meant changing his profession, changing
himself.

With that last line, the speaker becomes a man who sees
deeply into human feelings, one who understands the power
of pain, and one who states that understanding with the ut-
most simplicity. It is a simplicity, a symbolism, that reaches
out and down far beyond the apparent limits of the words,
themselves.

Prose-poetry

The final example is:

QUEST
Always when I see Italian marble
and great burnished mahogany sitting quiet
and ruthless in the indulgence of five centuries,

always I ask whose is the skull
set in jewels grinning there in shadow
who thrust all this from him feverishly
as the white dove flew nimbly from the mouth
and the feathers made great onslaughts
against the mind, loosening, flattening himself
to dive into the eye of the needle.

—Edwin Honig

Here is poetry based on metaphor. The phrase "Italian marble/
and great burnished mahogany sitting quiet/and ruthless in the
indulgence of five centuries" not only sets the tone for the
entire selection, but indicates clearly the metaphorical means
the poet is using. How can Italian marble and mahogany be
ruthless? How can the centuries be indulgent? There is, of
course, no literal truth here. The marble and mahogany are
ruthless in the sense that they are untouched by, or are imper-
vious to, time. But there is an immediate contradiction. Time,
the five centuries, is indulgent. Time allows the marble and
mahogany to remain untouched. The two metaphors contra-
dict each other, yet blend into one over-all statement. There is
power in both the marble and mahogany and in the centuries.
Each sort of power is immense. Although it would seem that
one must vanquish the other, they remain interlocked. It is a
perfect stasis of forces.

Then, why *five* centuries? Why not six, or ten, or a thou-
sand? Well, to be precise, five centuries ago from the time of
this writing would make it the year 1466. Combine that time
with the place—*Italian* marble and mahogany. The Italy of
five centuries ago was the very heart of the Renaissance, that
amazing and violent surge of classicism that brought the
world many of its greatest glories in art and science. The
marble and mahogany, in other words, are examples of the
finest works of art of the Western world. Further, they are
examples of the incredible riches that were possessed by a
few persons at that time. They are mementoes of the vast
luxury that was possible for the few. It was a luxury with
almost barbaric overtones. The owner of this particular mar-

ble and mahogany for instance, had his skull set in jewels. (Or someone else did.) And the jewelled skull is in contrast with the classical beauty of the works of art.

Next comes the idea that the possessor of this wealth, faced with death, "thrust all this from him feverishly." Why "feverishly"? In haste, in fear of dying too encumbered by riches. The allusion to the Biblical admonition regarding the difficulty the wealthy have in reaching heaven makes this clear. Death is represented by "the white dove flew nimbly from the mouth." The white dove is a symbol for the spirit or soul, a soul that leaves the body easily, "nimbly." The sensation of dying is represented by "the feathers made great onslaughts against the mind." The combination of "feathers," "onslaughts," and "mind" constitutes one of those instances in which the poet has made a choice that is perfectly right. The description of the feathers, the wings, of the soul beating against the mind and shattering it, is, in a word, poetry.

The speaker observes all this. He observes it from the point of view of today. He is not only aware of the ideas and emotions involved here, he is aware in a new way or in a deeper way.

Notice, in the above paragraphs, the awkwardness and the wordiness necessary for the "translation" of the poetry into nonpoetry. The speaker has, in a sense, created new language. It is impossible to say what he meant except by using the words he uses. Any paraphrase, necessary as it may be, is, at best, only an approximation of the speaker's meaning.

The selection is poetry, but it is *not* verse. Typographically, it looks like verse, but there is no rhythmic pattern involved. If the lines were run margin to margin, as

> Always when I see Italian marble and great burnished mahogany sitting quiet and ruthless in the indulgence of five centuries, always, etc.,

we would instantly call it prose. And since rhythm is not a visual phenomenon, the selection remains prose even though it is set in lines of arbitrary length. This speaker, then, has not imposed the burden of form on himself.

The setting is vague. It is one in which the speaker can contemplate, can feel without distraction. So it is apparently a quiet, familiar place.

Again, there is no particular audience indicated. The feelings expressed, the newness of meaning, belong to those who will take them.

In sum, this speaker is a person of our time, speaking in a peaceful setting, who feels himself a part of all things, including the past. He is impressed by people, not by things. He wonders how the possessors of riches live with those riches. And he wonders how they die with them. He is, perhaps, fearful of the burden of things, and this fearfulness, this desire for freedom, may be reflected in the lack of verse form.

Summary

The above are examples of the basic kinds of literature and of the speakers one encounters therein. These speakers differ from one another in ways that are always significant and sometimes extreme. The reader's job is to discover, to create these speakers, using the tools and techniques provided by the material. Since the speakers differ, the reader's reaction to and relationship with these speakers will differ, too. The next chapter will deal with that relationship.

CHAPTER SEVEN

The reader-speaker relationship

THE POINT of this whole business, the reason for saying all that has been said so far, lies primarily in the relationship between the reader and the speaker. As stated at the end of Chapter Four, the speaker is the goal, the core of the entire process, but speakers exist in dramatic contexts of "what," "where," "when," and "how," and, therefore, these dramatic elements are of great importance. The reader-speaker relationship is a relationship between a real person and an imaginary one, but it is, nonetheless, a real relationship. The reader has created this person, the speaker, and he must react to, respond to, in a sense *become*, the speaker.

As was mentioned earlier, to paraphrase a piece of literature is to distort it. The only way to say what the speaker said is to use the words the speaker used. Further, when he uses those words, the reader must mean by them what the speaker meant. And to use the speaker's words with the speaker's meaning is to *be*, to *become*, in one very important sense, the speaker.

The intellectual aspect

One of the fundamental aspects of the reader-speaker relationship is the fact that it is not *solely* an intellectual one.[29] There certainly may be important intellectual elements present. The reader may agree with the ideas, the viewpoints, the philosophy of the speaker. And those factors may bring pleasure to the reader. But if the reader insists on intellectual or rational agreement with all speakers, he immediately restricts himself, first, to that literature that has a logical or intellectual viewpoint, and second, to that literature with the ideas of which he agrees. Of course, the thought that readers should base their appreciation of literature on more than logic and reason is far from new. The new element here is that a person is involved—the speaker. And to discard or ignore speakers because one doesn't agree with them is, on one level, the same as discarding or ignoring real people because one doesn't agree with them. (The fact that some persons react to those around them in precisely this fashion does not make it less unfortunate.)

Consider this stanza from *The Rubaiyat*:

> And much as Wine has played the Infidel,
>   And robbed me of my Robe of Honour—Well,
> I often wonder what the Vintners buy
>   One half so precious as the stuff they sell.
>   —*Omar Khayyám*
>   *translated by Edward Fitzgerald*

The speaker here is openly singing the glories of wine. To those who themselves disapprove of drinking, the factual content herein is unacceptable. And it would be easy for such readers to understand this speaker to be saying "let's all get drunk"—period. Familiarity with the entire selection, the entire speaker, would make it quite clear that much more is involved. Even this excerpt, however, contains far more than "let's get drunk." The speaker personalizes wine, he makes of it an antagonist and a friend—a thing that is "precious" but that can steal his "robe of honour." Here is something to be treated with care, something of great value and danger. The reader who refuses to, or is unable to "meet" this speaker and accept him is limiting himself needlessly. It is perfectly possi-

ble to understand, appreciate, and derive pleasure from such
a speaker's attitudes and feelings without agreeing with them.
Here is another such case:

WOMAN
A clever man builds a city,
A clever woman lays one low;
With all her qualifications, that clever woman
Is but an ill-omened bird.
A woman with a long tongue
Is a flight of steps leading to calamity;
For disorder does not come from heaven,
But is brought about by women.
Among those who cannot be trained or taught
Are women and eunuchs.

*—From the Shi King, or
Book of Odes, compiled
by Confucius about 500 B.C.,
translated by H.A. Giles*

Despite the extremity of this speaker's views, there may be
a few readers who will agree with them. But certainly most
readers will not. How, then, may one disagree with the ideas
expressed here and still accept this speaker and enjoy the material? First of all, the speaker of this selection is not voicing
disdain, or mild contempt, or irritation, or ordinary disap-
proval. His condemnation of women is so sweepingly thorough that there is a sort of grandeur in that very fact. For
him, women are capable of all evils. Nothing, no misdeed, is
beyond their talents. But notice that this extreme view makes
of women malevolent angels or satanic saints. They are apparently supremely powerful, since they succeed in undoing
man's good works. And they are immune to teaching, even by
man. Finally, there seems to be a large amount of this sinister
femininity in man, for when he is turned into a eunuch, he
becomes, like women, untrainable and unteachable. This is a
far cry from a statement about women drivers, or feminine
illogic, or the devouring dependency of females; those state-

ments could be intended as factual or accurate; the one made
by this speaker has little to do with fact. It is exaggerated to
the nth degree. It might be called hyperbole, but it is almost
beyond that—almost hyperbolic hyperbole.

Combine this far-outness with the dramatic elements—the
setting some unspecified foreign country (the author's name
pinpoints it), the time the distant past, the form, verse (based
on the repetition of long phrases)—and it is quite clear that
there is no immediacy, no objective fact, no reality involved
here. The entire context is artificial, especially for today's
readers. To accept that artificiality is to allow one's self to
accept the speaker without having to agree with him. To insist on agreement is to consider the work as a factual statement, to ignore the artificiality.

For those who find the above examples too obvious, here is
one that is far more complex and closer to home for most of
us:

From JOHN BROWN'S BODY

There were three stout pillars that held up all
The weight and tradition of Wingate Hall.
One was Cudjo and one was you
And the third was the mistress, Mary Lou.
Mary Lou Wingate, as slightly made
And as hard to break as a rapier-blade.
Bristol's daughter and Wingate's bride,
Never well since the last child died
But staring at pain with courteous eyes.
When the pain outwits it, the body dies,
Meanwhile the body bears the pain.
She loved her hands and they made her vain,
The tiny hands of her generation
That gathered the reins of the whole plantation;
The velvet sheathing the steel demurely
In the trained, light grip that holds so surely.

She was at work by candlelight,
She was at work in the dead of night,

Smoothing out troubles and healing schisms
And doctoring phthisics and rheumatisms,
Guiding the cooking and watching the baking,
The sewing, the soap-and-candle making,
The brewing, the darning, the lady-daughters,
The births and deaths in the negro-quarters,
Seeing that Suke had some new, strong shoes
And Joe got a week in the calaboose,
While Dicey's Jacob escaped a whipping
And the jellybag dripped with its proper dripping,
And the shirts and estrangements were neatly mended,
And all of the tasks that never ended.

Her manner was gracious but hardly fervent
And she seldom raised her voice to a servant.
She was often mistaken, not often blind,
And she knew the whole duty of womankind,
To take the burden and have the power
And seem like the well-protected flower,
To manage a dozen industries
With a casual gesture in scraps of ease,
To hate the sin and to love the sinner
And to see that the gentlemen got their dinner
Ready and plenty and piping-hot
Whether you wanted to eat or not.
And always, always, to have the charm
That makes the gentlemen take your arm
But never the bright, unseemly spell
That makes strange gentlemen love too well,
Once you were married and settled down
With a suitable gentleman of your own.
And when that happened, and you had bred
The requisite children, living and dead,
To pity the fool and comfort the weak
And always let the gentlemen speak,
To succor your love from deep-struck roots
When gentlemen went to bed in their boots,
And manage a gentleman's whole plantation
In the manner befitting your female station.

This was the creed that her mother taught her
And the creed that she taught to every daughter.
She knew her Bible—and how to flirt
With a swansdown fan and a brocade skirt.
For she trusted in God but she liked formalities
And the world and Heaven were both realities.
—In Heaven, of course, we should all be equal,
But, until we came to that golden sequel,
Gentility must keep to gentility
Where God and breeding had made things stable,
While the rest of the cosmos deserved civility
But dined in its boots at the second table.
This view may be reckoned a trifle narrow,
But it had the driving force of an arrow,
And it helped Mary Lou to stand up straight,
For she was gentle, but she could hate
And she hated the North with the hate of Jael
When the dry hot hands went seeking the nail,
The terrible hate of women's ire,
The smoky, the long-consuming fire.
The Yankees were devils, and she could pray,
For devils, no doubt, upon Judgement Day,
But now in the world, she would hate them still
And send the gentlemen out to kill.

The gentlemen killed and the gentlemen died,
But she was the South's incarnate pride
That mended the broken gentlemen
And sent them out to the war again,
That kept the house with the men away
And baked the bricks when there was no clay,
Made courage from terror and bread from bran
And propped the South on a swansdown fan
Through four long years of ruin and stress,
The pride—and the deadly bitterness.

Let us look at her now, let us see her plain,
She will never be quite like this again.
Her house is rocking under the blast

And she hears it tremble, and still stands fast,
But this is the last, this is the last,
The last of the wine and the white corn meal,
The last high fiddle singing the reel,
The last of the silk with the Paris label,
The last blood-thoroughbred safe in the stable
—Yellow corn meal and a jackass colt,
A door that swings on a broken bolt,
Brittle old letters spotted with tears
And a wound that rankles for fifty years—
This is the last of Wingate Hall,
The last bright August before the Fall,
Death has been near, and Death has passed,
But this is the last, this is the last.
There will be hope, and a scratching pen,
There will be cooking for tired men,
The waiting for news with shut, hard fists,
And the blurred, strange names in the battle lists,
The April sun and the April rain,
But never this day come back again.

But she is lucky, she does not see
The axe-blade sinking into the tree
Day after day, with a slow, sure stroke
Till it chops the mettle from Wingate oak.
The house is busy, the cups are filling
To welcome the gentlemen back from killing,
The hams are boiled, and the chickens basting,
Fat Aunt Bess is smiling and tasting,
Cudjo's napkin is superfine,
He knows how the gentlemen like their wine,
Amanda is ready, Louisa near her,
Glistering girls from a silver mirror,
Everyone talking, everyone scurrying,
Upstairs and downstairs, laughing and hurrying,
Everyone giving and none denying,
There is only living, there is no dying.
War is a place but it is not here,
The peace and the victory are too near.
One more battle, and Washington taken,

The Yankees mastered, the South unshaken,
Fiddlers again, and the pairing season,
The old-time rhyme and the old-time reason,
The grandchildren, and the growing older
Till at last you need a gentleman's shoulder,
And the pain can stop, for the frayed threads sever,
But the house and the courtesy last forever.
—*Stephen Vincent Benét*

There are at least two basic ideas or attitudes that the speaker of this *excerpt* (familiarity with the entire work will change the reader-speaker relationship considerably) is expressing that will be difficult for many readers to accept.

The first is the attitude toward Negroes. There is no pretense of equality between Negroes and whites. And the fact that Mary Lou found many people, not only Negroes, inferior, offers little help. The speaker describes her attitude as "a trifle narrow," but adds that it had "all the driving force of an arrow." He does not condemn her for it. Today, with the very strong feelings that exist about the Civil Right's movement, the very lack of condemnation will make this offensive to some readers. There is certainly nothing mysterious about this. When one is involved in a realistically painful situation it is obviously difficult, at best, to respond to a piece of literature that reminds one of that pain. For example, to ask a Negro who is the target of discrimination in housing, employment, education, etc., to understand and appreciate this selection is asking a great deal, indeed. But that is exactly what must be asked. In no sense are Negroes being singled out as a group that must make special literary efforts. The other side of this particular coin is that the white Southern or Northern racist must be asked to understand and appreciate the deep melancholy and the cries of pain in much literature written by Negroes. And, of course, it includes all people, singly and in groups. One must be asked to understand the pride that Nazis and Facists took in their military strength. And one must be asked to respond appreciatively to it when it is represented in literature.

There is no question in any of these cases of agreeing with the point of view involved. Hopefully, readers will consider the pain inflicted on Negroes as a thing of horror, the totalitarian governments of World War II, instruments of terror. But, when represented in literature, and when there is no attempt or intent to secure agreement with an attitude or idea, these elements are secondary in importance to the human feelings presented. Mary Lou was a woman of great strength and graciousness who lived in a time of upheaval. It is her feelings that are important.

The second attitude of the speaker of the above excerpt has to do with the role of woman in society. Here, again, there is no pretense at equality. Women are to "always let the gentlemen speak," "seem like a well-protected flower," and "always, always to have the charm/That makes the gentlemen take your arm/But never the bright, unseemly spell/That makes strange gentlemen love too well." Mary Lou accepts this role, and the speaker accepts her acceptance of it. He does not make fun of her, or urge any change of views.

Few women today would be content with such a role, or would approve of a period in which women had to live such a life. And many women, for that reason, may find this speaker difficult to relate to. But, again, it is in no way necessary to agree that women are inferior to men in order to appreciate this selection. This is literature. It is not reality. And one must respond to the two on different bases.

Not only is Mary Lou unreal, but it is quite probable that the entire background of the piece is unreal. It's unlikely that the South was ever as it is pictured here, or that the social group pictured here ever existed, or that Southern women were like Mary Lou. But in one important sense, it makes no difference whether or not Mary Lou, or her background, was real. This is not history, but poetry, and the two are fundamentally different.[30] For factual or historical accuracy one reads history. The only accuracy or reality that is of basic importance in poetry, and in much nonpoetry, is an emotional reality. And Mary Lou's feelings and attitudes, together with those of the speaker and of the readers of this excerpt, are, or can be, very real, indeed. She "propped the South on a swans-down fan/Through four long years of ruin and stress." This statement is a key to Mary Lou and to the whole excerpt. It is certainly unreal in most, and perhaps all, objective senses. But there is a glitter to it—a kind of delicate strength—that makes it lovely, and that makes it quite possible to respond to the speaker, to Mary Lou, to the excerpt, without ever considering actual agreement with points of view expressed.

The emotional aspect

There is another issue that is closely related to the fact that the reader and the speaker need not agree intellectually. Putting it simply, it is that the reader and speaker need not agree emotionally. That is, the speaker may be a neurotic, a vicious person, a murderer, a coward, etc., but if he is speaking well, i.e., if the piece of literature is of worth, there will be some basis on which the reader can understand, accept, and respond to the speaker. It is a truism in clinical psychology that if the psychotherapist cannot empathize with the patient—cannot imaginatively put himself in the patient's frame of reference, cannot appreciate the beauty and the rewards the patient finds in even the most bizarre behavior—he will be of no help as a therapist. There are important similarities between the reader-speaker and the therapist-patient relationships. There are also, of course, important differences.

Basic to the therapist's attitude toward his patient is the clear-cut distinction he makes between feelings and acts. Certainly in all usual circumstances, one must exert a large degree of control over one's behavior, over one's acts. And quite often behavior is rewarded or punished by society, parents, friends, etc. To the psychotherapist, however, feelings are something quite different. By definition, feelings are neither good nor bad. They are, in varying degree, pleasurable or painful. But there is and can be nothing wrong, nothing evil, nothing bad in a feeling.

For example, and it is one that therapists encounter frequently, there is nothing wrong in feeling hostility toward one's parents. Even extreme hostility. Even to the extent of wanting to kill them. Few people without psychological training, and especially few parents, make this distinction. But, as stated, it is basic to the art of clinical psychology.

One of the major reasons on which psychotherapists base this separation of feelings and actions is the realization, acquired during their training, that we are all subject to roughly the same feelings. Differences in feelings occur from person to person, but they are primarily differences in degree, not in kind. This is an uncomfortable idea for many of us. The thought that the emotional drives of the psychotic are not necessarily very different from one's own is a sobering one. The emotional dividing line between the "normal" and the "abnormal," whatever those words mean, is certainly a thin one, if, indeed, it exists at all. And that very fact can be threatening to many of us. As long as we think of ourselves as comfortably and safely "normal," or fundamentally different from the neurotic or psychotic, we are protected. Protected from ourselves. That protection, of course, has a price, and it can be a high one. It can take the form, mentioned earlier, of forcing us to condemn and to avoid emotional contact with others. And it can take the even costlier form of forcing us to avoid emotional contact with ourselves, or with parts of ourselves. If, for instance, we feel that anger or hostility is ugly, or unacceptable, or frightening enough, we will be forced to disavow that very set of feelings in ourselves. And in so doing we become emotional cripples. Feeling anger is part of the human state. When that feeling becomes so threatening that we must hide it from ourselves, explain it away, etc., we are trying to put artificial limits on our emotional apparatus. We are trying to eliminate part of ourselves, and in the trying we are likely to distort a considerable amount, if not all, of the remainder of our emotional being.

The point of all this, in terms of the reader-speaker relationship, is that (1) as with intellectual agreement, if we insist on dealing only with those speakers who are "normal," or who are like us, or who are "good" people, we drastically limit our literary responses, and (2) there is a basis for responding to the speakers of literature that does not exist in life itself. That basis is the unreality of literature and its speakers. Whether or not one makes the fundamental distinction between feelings and actions in life, one can do so in literature. A real psychopath, or maniac, or depressive, may be very threatening, but speakers are not real people. They have no actual power over us. That fact makes it possible to respond to, let's say, a sadist in literature, while we may choose to avoid sadists in life. One might go so far as to say that accepting speakers of literature will make it possible to accept people in real life. Many therapists do use literature as an aid. But without considering this aspect of the thing, one can stress the literary rewards that acceptance of speakers will bring.

Here is an example of this difference between literature and life. The first of these two selections is a poem by a poet.

WITHOUT CEREMONY

Except ourselves, we have no other prayer;
Our needs are sores upon our nakedness.
We do not have to name them; we are here.
And You who can make eyes can see no less.
We fall, not on our knees, but on our hearts,
A posture humbler far and more downcast;
While Father Pain instructs us in the arts
Of praying, hunger is the worthiest fast.
We find ourselves where tongues cannot wage war
On silence (farther, mystics never flew)
But on the common wings of what we are,
Borne on the wings of what we bear, toward You,
Oh Word, in whom our wordiness dissolves,
When we have not a prayer except ourselves.
—*Vassar Miller*

The second is a letter from a patient to a therapist. It has been arranged into lines to make it visually analogous with the above selection.

Joyful am I when the Sun rises in the Dawn of time
And even more joyful when He rises in the Dawn of
    Eternity.
Even knowing it will set again in Time,
Just as He sets in Eternity,
For the end of the Day is not the end of Time,
Nor is the End of the World the End of Eternity.
There will be another Dawn and another
Always and forevermore.
In the beginning was Ego and Motion.
Ego and Motion became as one.
God and I became as one.
The World was born from Us.
Life was born unto Us.
Together God and I can walk the Earth;
Together we feel and think.
Apart we are the irresistible force and the immovable
    object.
In the beginning Ego thought only of itself,
Then Ego thought of God and Motion moved more
And Life became a greater thing.
And then Ego thought of Alter-Ego and His Motion
Moved them to walk the Earth.
We call this Love.
Love ye one another as I have loved you.

From the reader's viewpoint, one of the primary differences
between these selections is the fact that one speaker is unreal,
the other real. The poem may or may not reflect some significant part of its author's character or personality. The
reader certainly cannot assume that it does. This speaker,
then, bears no necessary relationship to the author or the
selection. The letter presumably does reflect important and
highly significant parts of its author's personality. Familiarity
with the case history involved would make it even clearer
that it does. One does not write a letter for the same reason
that one writes a poem.

The speaker of the letter and the reader are both real
people, and the contact between the two may be disturbing.

If each reader could be the actual recipient of the letter, the contact would certainly be disturbing for many. The reader of the poem is real, but the speaker of the poem is unreal. Contact beween these two need not be threatening.

The fact is that many of us have experienced many of the feelings experienced by the speakers of each of these selections. In the poem, the frustrating futility of words, the feeling of some vague, unnameable need, are familiar to us. In the letter, the blurring of reality and unreality, the feeling of being beyond ordinary forces, of being one with the universe, are also familiar. The only thing that would make the feelings expressed in the poem acceptable and those expressed in the letter unacceptable is the fact that the reader knows that the speaker of the letter is a real person. Suppose that the letter had been given a title and labeled poetry. The reader would then have been forced to approach these two selections, these two speakers, on exactly the same basis. He would have had to consider them as literature. They differ, of course, in terms of literary worth. Nevertheless, both are built on metaphorical language. Neither has much to do with factual, objective truth. Both deal with subjective truth, and both use language in much the same way to express this truth. Shakespeare's statement, "The lunatic, the lover, and the poet are of imagination all compact" is, perhaps, appropriate here in the sense that both the poet and the emotionally disturbed person must use metaphorical language to express themselves. But the reader knows that the letter was written by an emotionally disturbed person only because he was told that fact. Had he been told that the writer of the letter was a poet, he would have had to approach it in precisely the same way he would approach the poem, i.e., via its speaker.

As Frye pointed out, direct address has no place in literature. As long as one considers the letter as a statement by a real person, there is a too direct contact between that person and the reader, and that contact can be quite disturbing. As soon as one considers it as literature, as a statement by a speaker, there is a safety factor that is involved. No contact occurs between the reader and the author; instead, there is an in-between element, the speaker, that allows the reader to become aware of a segment of reality that remains safely distant, and, in a sense, unreal. The test of the material, then, is whether or not it functions as literature—whether or not it uses some means, metaphor in this case, to create an emotionally pleasurable response.

One of the rewards to be found in accepting speakers such as the ones in these selections, in accepting literature of this sort, is the fact that we can emotionally relax and experience, and, via performance, express, feelings that we may have had to ignore, repress, suppress, etc. Consider the first three lines of the poem:

> Except ourselves, we have no other prayer;
> Our needs are sores upon our nakedness.
> We do not have to name them; we are here.

The meanings contained in these lines are multifold. "We are, I am, prayer. All our wants are visible. They cannot be hidden. And they constitute our prayers. Naming them is useless; their existence is more powerful than any label. All prayers in words are artificial. We cannot avoid our illnesses, our faults, and, therefore, we cannot avoid prayer." These, and more, meanings are involved in these first lines. But for many of us, particularly for the nonreligiously oriented, some of these thoughts and feelings may seem unacceptable in reality. Here, however, is a speaker, an unreal person, who expresses these feelings, and we can share them with him without running the risks involved in sharing them with a real person.

Now consider these lines from the letter, *treating it as literature:*

> In the beginning was Ego and Motion.
> Ego and Motion became as one.
> God and I became as one.
> The world was born from Us.
> Life was born unto Us.

Together God and I can walk the Earth;
Apart we are the irresistable force and the immovable
    object.
In the beginning Ego thought only of itself,
Then Ego thought of God and Motion moved more
And Life became a greater thing.
And then Ego thought of Alter-Ego and His Motion
Moved them to walk the Earth.

There is a strange but effective pairing of "Ego and Motion"
and "God and I." Apparently, Ego stands for God, and Motion for the speaker. It might seem more appropriate to pair
them in the reverse order. But the concept of God as Ego
and the "I," perhaps standing for mankind, as Motion has a
poetic value. The term Ego is conventionally used as one of
the elements in the human personality. In this context, it
seems to indicate that God is an element, a basic element, in
a total personality of which man is a part. Motion, movement,
activity, as symbol for man is an interesting choice. If there
is anything that is basic to the human condition, it would
seem to be movement—movement of all sorts, on all levels,
in all directions. Combine this with Ego, and a picture
emerges of a personality, the central part of which is a fixed,
unmoving, stable God, with man constituting the moving,
changing periphery.

This sort of meaning is involved and abstruse, but there is
at least some literary value here. However, notice what happens a little further on:

In the beginning Ego thought only of itself,
Then Ego thought of God and Motion moved more
And Life became a greater thing.
And then Ego thought of Alter-Ego and His Motion
Moved them to walk the Earth.

These lines are cloudy and unclear. In addition to the pairing
of "Ego and Motion" with "God and I," there is now the
statement "Ego thought of God." It doesn't seem to fit. How

did Ego exist before or without God? Then the element Alter-Ego. What is symbolized here? The devil? Evil? Next, the words "His Motion" seem to refer to Alter-Ego. Another contradictory or confusing factor. From the relatively effective matching of "Ego and Motion" with "God and I," the selection has moved to a point at which Ego, Motion, God, I, Alter-Ego, and His Motion form a confusing, blurred, fragmented word-jumble. The thing begins to fail as literature. But that is all that is involved—literary failure. If one were to approach this material as a letter, the confusion in the last lines might be uncomfortable to deal with. As reality, this is schizophrenia. As literature, it is merely ineffective. And the reader need react only to that ineffectiveness, not to the schizophrenia.

Here is an especially interesting example of a speaker who, like the lover in Shakespeare's trio, is both lunatic and poet:

THE LOVELY SHALL BE CHOOSERS
The Voice said, "Hurl her down!"

The Voices, "How far down?"

"Seven levels of the world."

"How much time have we?"

"Take twenty years.
She *would* refuse love safe with wealth and honor!
The lovely shall be choosers, shall they?
Then let them choose!"

"Then we shall let her choose?"

"Yes, let her choose.
Take up the task beyond her choosing."

Invisible hands crowded on her shoulder
In readiness to weigh upon her.
But she stood straight still,
In broad round ear-rings, gold and jet with pearls
And broad round suchlike brooch,
Her cheeks high colored,
Proud and the pride of friends.

The Voice asked, "You can let her choose?"

"Yes, we can let her and still triumph."

"Do it by joys, and leave her always blameless.
Be her first joy her wedding,
That though a wedding,
Is yet—well something they know, he and she.
And after that her next joy
That though she grieves, her grief is secret:
Those friends know nothing of her grief to make it
    shameful.
Her third joy that though now they cannot help but
    know,
They move in pleasure too far off
To think much or much care.
Give her a child at either knee for fourth joy
To tell once and once only, for them never to forget,
How once she walked in brightness,
And make them see it in the winter firelight.
But give her friends for then she dare not tell
For their forgone incredulousness.
And be her next joy this:
Her never having deigned to tell them.
Make her among the humble even
Seem to them less than they are.
Hopeless of being known for what she has been,
Failing of being loved for what she is,
Give her the comfort for her sixth of knowing
She fails from strangeness to a way of life
She came to from too high too late to learn.
Then send some *one* with eyes to see
And wonder at her where she is,
And words to wonder in her hearing how she came there,
But without time to linger for her story.
Be her last joy her heart's going out to this one
So that she almost speaks.

You know them—seven in all."

"Trust us," the Voices said.

—*Robert Frost*

One of the first things that will strike those readers familiar with Frost's works is the fact that this selection is so "unlike" Frost. Where is the kindly, gentle, perhaps a bit detached, philosopher? The observer of human pain and weakness? For those who insist on finding the author in each and every one of his works, this selection can be troublesome. It might send them scurrying to biographies to find out whether or not Frost had an unfortunate love affair some time in the past. And if he didn't, what then? Using the concept of a speaker, all this is unnecessary. This speaker has no necessary relationship to Robert Frost.

This speaker is, of course, vengeful. He wishes for another human being the most extreme and consistent agony. Not some quick burst of pain, but a long, subtle, and unavoidable series of hurts. One of the cultural commandments of our time, to which we pay emotional lip service, at least, is that we should not feel the need for vengeance. But who among us has not felt the desire for revenge in some way, perhaps in a way quite similar to that expressed by the speaker of this work? Here, then, is an opportunity to let down these particular emotional bars, and to experience with this speaker the feeling of wishing great ill to another. In reality we may choose to deny such feelings, but this is not reality, and, therefore, there is no need to deny them.

More specifically, this speaker wishes all this suffering on a woman, a lovely woman, who chose another. The fury of a woman scorned has been described in all sorts of writings. Here is the fury of a man scorned. This speaker hates. Clearly, his anger and hatred could be appropriately called abnormal, neurotic, unrealistic, etc., from one point of view. But are we not all familiar with this feeling? Aren't we all "abnormal" in some degree when it comes to love? Exploring a little more deeply, do not all men, even the most "normal," feel some edge of fear or anger at a woman who has great beauty? In our culture, beauty is power, and power, even when not used, is threatening. This speaker is really blaming the woman for possessing that power. It is her fault that she is lovely.

THE READER-SPEAKER RELATIONSHIP

Imagine this selection being written about an ugly woman—
"The Ugly Shall Be Choosers." The whole thing becomes
silly. The speaker is angry at the woman's loveliness, and is
actually feeling that her loveliness is a personal attack on him.
As a feeling, one may label it neurotic, or whatever, but is it
not a commonplace and familiar one? We may choose to
avoid these feelings in reality, but this speaker is unreal. There
is no need to avoid them here. There is, instead, the
pleasure that can come from admitting and experiencing, in
a safely unreal situation, feelings that we all possess.

More specifically still, this speaker hears voices and talks
to them. They are apparently able and willing to carry out
his wishes. In reality this might be considered paranoia. But,
first, this is literature, not reality, and, second, are we not all
a bit paranoid in this sense? Don't we all wish, at times, that
fate, or destiny, or the powers that be, would take our side,
would punish our enemies? Is there anyone who has not, at
some time, wanted godlike powers, and wanted them for the
purpose of controlling, of bringing pain and pleasure to others? Here, again, is material that allows us to express feelings
we have all experienced, and to do so in a context that re-
moves the threat that normally accompanies them.

Summary

As stated at the beginning of this chapter, the reader creates
the speaker and he must then become, in a sense, that speaker.
It is a very real sense in which this happens, but it is *a sense*
only. If the author has performed his task well and has dealt
with attitudes and feelings that are or can be familiar to the
reader, the reader, if he is to perform well, must allow himself to respond, to re-experience the feelings stirred up by the
material. In doing so he becomes the speaker in a real sense.
The feelings he experiences are real feelings. Obviously, however, there is no question of a total or basic personality change
involved here. The reader does not become an actual whim-
pering child, or depressed old man, etc. In becoming the

speaker, the reader simply permits himself to express one group of the vast complex of feelings that make up his emotional being, even though he might not permit himself that freedom of expression in other circumstances.

CHAPTER EIGHT

The reader-speaker—audience relationship

❧

THE odd-looking title of this chapter is meant to indicate that the reader can, in the sense previously discussed, become the speaker, and that what is to be considered now is the relationship between the speaker part of the reader and the audience part of the reader, and between the speaker part of the reader and an audience of other persons, if there is one. In other words, at this stage the reader becomes two people, a reader-speaker and a reader-audience, and, therefore, there is now a relationship between these two people, and between the reader-speaker and any further audience.

These relationships are fundamentally the same in that both involve the performing, the expressing of feelings and attitudes that are *part* of the reader and are appropriate for, are *all* of, the speaker. They may differ, in degree, in that the performance for an audience of other persons will be explicit, detailed, and consistent, while the performance for the audience part of the reader will often be somewhat abridged, less overt, implicit. It is of vital importance, however, that the reader-speaker be able to use the same thoroughgoing, detailed performance techniques in performing for himself, for the reader-audience, that he would use in performing for an audience of others. He may need to use them only occasionally, but when the need arises, those techniques are just as important, if not more so, for the reader-audience as for an audience of other people.

It was stated in the Introduction that the goal of oral interpretation is the realization of, the participation in, literature, and that this goal necessarily involves performance for one's self, but not performance for others. The oralization of literature is the basis of this process, and for that oralization the only requisite audience is the reader-audience. Further, in order to perform well for an audience of others, the reader-speaker must be able to perform for himself, for the reader-audience. This is analogous to Frye's statement that one must be able to speak well if one is to be able to read or write well. From the point of view of this text, one must be able to speak well to one's self if one is to be able to speak well to others.

General performance techniques

All the kinds of performance behaviour that the reader-speaker uses for an audience of others can, and, at times, must, be used for the reader-audience. Performance behavior can be divided into two categories, *voice*, meaning any and all ways in which the performer uses his voice, and *movement*, meaning any and all ways in which the performer uses his body. Although the specific techniques that make up these kinds of behavior are the same whether the reader-speaker is performing for the reader-audience or for an audience of others, those techniques have different subjective values depending on whether the point of view taken is that of the reader-speaker, the reader-audience, or an audience of others.

For example, for the reader-speaker, all movement has primarily a physiological or kinesthetic value. He feels his body move, his muscles act. For an audience of others, all movement has a visual appeal. They see the reader-speaker move. In addition, there is the empathic response that is based on muscular imitation, and that leads to emotional imitation that allows the audience to feel what the reader-speaker is feeling. So that, for an audience of others, movement has, first, a visual appeal, and, second, a kinesthetic appeal.

For the reader-audience, movement is a strange combination of the above viewpoints. The reader-audience feels the reader-speaker's movement, i.e., there is a kinesthetic value. But he may also visualize, from an imagined outside vantage point, that movement. He may, figuratively, stand off and watch himself, or the other part of himself, in performance. There is, then, visual appeal of a sort involved. And in imaginatively observing himself, the reader-audience may respond to the reader-speaker, not on a simple muscular level, but on what might be called a psychomuscular level. It is as if, seeing the movement of the reader-speaker, the reader-audience responded in an appreciative sense to that movement. For the reader-audience, then, movement has kinesthetic, visual, and, let's say, esthetic values.

With voice, the differences are less marked. For the reader-speaker, all vocal techniques have primarily auditory values. He hears himself speaking. In addition, there is the physiological aspect referred to earlier. He feels his muscles producing the words. For an audience of others, voice is also primarily auditory in value, although there is an esthetic appeal, based on vocal quality and diction, that is interwoven with the auditory. For the reader-audience, voice involves auditory, physiological (he feels the reader-speaker's muscles articulate), and esthetic appeals. The last element exists when the reader-audience looks on, observes in the sense mentioned above. Voice, then, is from all viewpoints primarily auditory. For the reader-speaker, it involves values that are auditory and physiological, for the audience of others, auditory and esthetic values, and for the reader-audience, auditory, physiological, and esthetic values.

Acting versus interpretation

Before discussing the specific techniques the reader-speaker uses, there is one problem that requires comment. It is a problem that, in this writer's opinion, has been created by theorists in the area. As mentioned in the Introduction, oral interpretation is conventionally considered in terms of performance by a reader for an audience of others. And the kind of performance called oral interpretation is described or defined as differing from the kind of performance called acting. The usual statement of the difference goes something like this: *The actor "presents";* he tries to make the audience believe he *is* the character whose lines he speaks; he uses much more varied vocal and bodily behavior; he has, ordinarily, theatrical aids such as costume, make-up, lighting, etc., to work with. On the other hand, *the interpreter "represents";* he does not try to make the audience believe he *is* a given character, but *suggests* that character in such a way that both he and the audience can observe and appreciate; his vocal and bodily behavior is relatively restrained or understated; usually, he has few technical aids to work with.[31]

On one level, this seems a plausible enough distinction. The performer who shouts Othello's rage against a theatrical background of lighting, costume, make-up, scenery, etc., is an actor. The performer who quietly reads a lyric poem by John Ciardi in a lighted classroom is an interpreter. This text, however, will take the view that there is no fundamental difference between these two performances. They may differ in many ways, but the differences will always be in degree, not in kind.

One way to approach this idea is to begin with the actor, the performer doing Othello, and to remove one element at a time. First, imagine that the scenery has been removed. Then the lighting. The costume. The make-up, etc. Finally, there is a performer standing in street dress, reading from a manuscript in a fairly controlled fashion. At what point did he stop being an actor and become something else? Or begin at the other end. To the interpreter doing a Ciardi lyric, add one element at a time. Lighting, costume, movement, etc. When did he stop interpreting and start acting? It seems to this writer that there is simply no point at which one can say, "This is acting, but this is interpreting." The two performances, then, exist on a continuum. All basic performance elements present in one are present in the other; they will vary only in amount, in quantity. Those elements that can be totally removed or added are not basic performance elements. It is foolish to say, for instance, that an actor cannot act without make-up, or costume, or lighting. These factors are not necessary characteristics of acting, and the absence of these elements is not a necessary characteristic of oral interpretation. When one eliminates these factors and considers only the elements basic to the act or nature of performance, one deals with the performer's use of his voice and body. And the actor and the interpreter differ in no fundamental fashion in this area. Even the existence of the two words, "acting" and "interpreting," is incongruous and misleading. The words exist, though, and are widely used. Therefore, this text will employ the terms to indicate differences in techniques used by the performer, and nothing else.

There is one further point to be made about the so-called difference between acting and interpreting. Consider the following phrases: "acting a part in a play," and "acting a poem, or short story, or essay." The first one, "acting a part in a play," is perfectly acceptable. One *can* act a part in a play. Why? Because there is a character to be acted. But the second, "acting a poem, or short story, or essay," sounds odd. Why? Because the assumption, though unstated, is that there is no character in these kinds of literature that can be acted. The problem, of course, disappears if one accepts the premise of this text: All literature is drama; behind every piece of literature there is a speaker. The speakers in conventional drama are simply more clearly or thoroughly revealed. The performer, be he actor or interpreter, attempts to become, to some degree, though never entirely, the speaker of the work with which he is dealing. It is just as possible, then, to perform—be it acting or interpreting—a poem or short story as a play. The performer will choose to act or interpret the work according to the demands made by his physical and psychological environment.

Many years ago, when this author was performing outside the classroom, an incident occurred on the stage of the Roxy Theater in New York. We were doing the dress rehearsal for a swashbuckling sort of number, in which we were replete with gold braid, boots, cloaks, etc. At one point it was necessary to make a movement to capture the audience's attention. I raised one arm, thinking that was enough of an attention catcher. The director stopped me and explained, in relatively profane terms, that it was nowhere near enough—that we were on an enormous stage—that from the balcony we were half-inch-high figures—and that I should make a quarter turn to one side, bend far over, catch one edge of the cloak, and turn back to the audience, flinging the cloak wide in a swirl of color. It seemed a grotesquely overdone movement to me, but it was necessary because of the unusual size of the house. In a small room it would be ridiculous.

Much of what the performer does results from demands made by his physical environment. An obvious example is volume. Another is tempo. In a large room, the performer must speak more loudly and slowly than in a small one. In fact, most, if not all, techniques the performer uses will have to be expanded or diminished in relation to the size of the performance area.

Very often the physical setting has the effect of separating the performer from the audience both physically and psychologically. Conventional staging, with footlights, difference in level between performer and audience, etc., has precisely this function. Any physical separation between performer and audience will tend to be a psychological separation also. And any psychological separation will allow the performer freedom to increase the size of the techniques he uses. This increase should be understood to include "lows" as well as "highs." That is, it is not a question of simply talking louder and faster, the greater the degree of separation. It is, rather, a question of talking more loudly *and* more softly, more rapidly *and* more slowly, etc., the greater the degree of separation. For example, motion pictures provide as great a degree of separation between performer and audience as is possible. To the physical factors of lighting, distance, etc., in the motion picture house is added the fact that the performers are not real people, but pictures of real people. This extreme separation makes it possible for the performer to bellow with rage or to whisper in fury, to race joyously down a street or to stand perfectly still with happiness. In another setting, say a classroom, *both* the bellow and the whisper, the racing and the stillness would be overdone.

The performer's psychological environment makes further demands on him. There are artistic and cultural conventions that can be ignored only at the performer's peril. For example, it was mentioned early in the text that it is conventional to read Shakespeare with a formal, precise sort of diction. If, for some reason, a performer chooses to read Shakespeare in informal, conversational speech, he'd better do something to let the audience know what to expect. Otherwise, there will be a clash between the expectation and the reality.

Theatrical trappings, lighting, costume, etc., lead audiences to expect the use of techniques this text calls acting. The absence of those trappings will create expectations of the techniques called interpretation. Certainly the performer may violate the audience's expectations, but he can never ignore them. In a situation in which the audience expects interpretation, the performer may begin by interpreting, then slowly move over toward acting. There may even be occasions on which the performer deliberately uses techniques the audience does not expect. If he is aware that those techniques are not expected, and if the resulting surprise works out to his advantage, well and good. If, through unawareness or poor artistic planning the results are detrimental to the performance, changes are clearly called for.

At this point, some happily skeptical reader may be thinking, "Well, if the only difference between acting and interpreting lies in the techniques used, why bother with the whole thing? Why not leave it all to the academic area called

Drama, especially since you say that all literature is drama anyway?"

It is a good question. The answer lies not in the nature of the performance involved, but in the nature and purpose of the two approaches to literature. Obviously there is some overlap between the academic fields of Drama and Oral Interpretation. There are, however, greater differences than likenesses. Most of the time, in some cases all the time, students in Drama study plays. Students in Oral Interpretation study all literary forms. Most of the time, in some cases all the time, students in Drama are oriented toward performance before an actual audience. Students in Oral Interpretation have as their primary goal the understanding and appreciation of literature, and only intermittently and secondarily actual performance before an audience of others.

Putting it briefly, the area of Drama concentrates almost entirely on plays and is geared primarily for conventional performance. It would, therefore, seem to belong to the Fine Arts. Oral Interpretation is a tool of literary inquiry, including all literary forms, and having actual performance as a secondary goal, at most. It would, therefore, seem to belong to the Humanities.

Specific performance techniques

In discussing specific performance techniques, the point made in the Introduction should be kept in mind. As a whole, these techniques are neither totally predetermined patterns of behavior nor spontaneous responses to the material.[32] They are both. Some of the techniques may be planned in advance. Others may occur spontaneously. But with both the ones that are planned and the ones that are not, actual performance may disclose problems. One may plan to read a particular part of a selection in a high, plaintive voice, and find that doing so does not feel right, does not achieve the desired effect. Or one may find that spontaneous techniques are too irregular and undependable with certain material, and one may, therefore, plan to use specific kinds of vocal and bodily behavior. In other words, everything that follows should be understood to mean that there are no rules, *per se*, but that general principles exist and should be carefully studied and used.

Beginning with movement, probably the simplest aspect thereof is posture. But though simple, posture is extremely important. The reader-speaker who, because of his posture, gives an impression of poise, alertness, strength, and control furnishes himself (the reader-audience) and the audience of others with a basis for an emphatic response. The reader-speaker who seems to droop dispiritedly and disinterestedly is likely to provoke a similar audience response. Around the beginning of this century, a writer in this field, S. S. Curry, talked of the importance of posture.[33] He advocated an erect stance, with the weight slightly forward on one foot, and the chest raised. To adopt this posture as a permanent, rigid requirement would make for a mechanical approach to performance. But if one considers it as a physical norm, a "rest position" from which he may depart at any time, a standard against which all movement may be measured, it may be an effective technique. Such posture is likely to give an impression of controlled strength. It must be emphasized, however, that one may leave this rest position at any point, assuming that there is some reason or purpose for doing so, returning to it when that purpose has been satisfied.

Eye contact is another important aspect of movement. Unless he is doing so for some particular effect, the reader-speaker should not look out the window, or at the floor or ceiling. He should look at, *or pretend to look at,* an audience, whether or not there is an actual audience present. The italicized phrase is important because there are many, many times when looking into the eyes of members of a real audience can be most distracting. The concept of the necessary indirectness of literature is related to this performance technique. The reader-speaker should never use eye contact or any other technique so much, or in such a way, as to bring the actual audience too close to the reader as a person. Contact is made between the reader-speaker and the audience of others, not between the reader as a person and that audience. Especially with intensely emotional material (a delicate love lyric, a cry of protest or pain), direct eye contact is unwanted. For instance, the reader who does Elizabeth Barrett Browning's "How Do I Love Thee" looking straight at the members of the audience will succeed only in making them, and himself, uncomfortable. With such material, one must give the impression of looking at the audience while never actually catching individuals' eyes. With a little practice, the knack of looking between the members of the audience, but at the audience as a whole, is easily mastered.

Gestures may or may not be used. Most of us find it easy to use few or no gestures, difficult to use them often. For that simple reason, the inexperienced reader-speaker should probably force himself to use a few more gestures than he would like.

"Repetitive" gestures, that is, gestures that say the same thing the words say, should ordinarily be avoided. Pointing up for the word "up," or down for "down," shading one's eyes for "see," are examples. (Such gestures may be suitable in comic material.)

Gestures should be completed. Because we are not thoroughly at ease with gestures, we often start them, then cut them off in the middle. Lifting and spreading the arms can be a descriptive gesture indicating hugeness, limitlessness, etc. But if the arms are half lifted, then quickly dropped, the effect is completely ruined, and attention is drawn to the distracting gesture rather than to the meaning of the words. It is far better to complete a gesture that is, perhaps, ill-chosen than to leave half finished the most appropriate of gestures.

Facial expressions are probably the most important part of movement. They are certainly the most difficult part to deal with directly. Facial movements are so variable, so fleeting, and so subtle that it is practically impossible to deliberately use one or more of them without seeming mechanical and artificial. Instead, concentration on the total meaning of the words, absorption in the feeling of the material, is a far more dependable way of insuring that facial expressions will be effective and appropriate.

Possibly the simplest aspect of voice is tempo, the amount of time spent in speaking the actual words and in pausing between the words. Most beginners read too rapidly with too few pauses. Tempo, of course, will vary with varying materials. But, generally speaking, the inexperienced should read more slowly than they think normal or suitable. Most especially, beginning readers should pause far, far more than they feel is usual. Pauses are one of the most effective ways of drawing attention to a word, or thought, or phrase. Pauses can highlight a piece of material. Used well, a pause is not merely a piece of dead time. It is a period in which suspense or anticipation is quickened, or in which feelings already expressed are allowed to grow, to feed upon themselves.

A somewhat more complex aspect of auditory behavior is the use of volume and pitch. The two can be considered separately, but in performance they normally go together, i.e., a change in one involves a change in the other. There is nothing more deadly than a reading that drones along on one monotonous level of volume and pitch, particularly if the tempo is also steady and unvaried. Variety is the key word. Volume and pitch should be varied far beyond what the average beginning reader thinks of as acceptable. Changes in these elements can be used to separate one thought from another, to indicate primary versus subordinate phrases or ideas, to underline or emphasize the emotional peaks and valleys of the material, and, of course, to keep the audience awake, alert, and interested.

Probably the most complicated aspect of auditory behavior is diction. As used here, it is a general term meaning any and all of the ways in which words can be uttered—formally, informally, with various accents, or in various dialects, softly and pleadingly, brusquely and angrily, explosively, etc. Some of these items are traditionally considered to be outside the realm of diction, but to this writer they are impossible to separate. In reading a Damon Runyan short story, for instance, how can one detach the Brooklynese dialect from the elements of humor and pathos that the use of that dialect produces? Or with a Noel Coward play, how can the British accent, if it is used, be separated from the feeling of restraint and understatement that it elicits?

Certain elements of diction are more familiar, and, therefore, easier than others for most of us. We are at home with conversational, sloppy diction, less so with formal, precise diction, at ease with our own particular dialect, uncomfortable with others, etc. Obviously, then, one must take care to match the diction to the material even if it means making the performance more difficult. Further, one must spend more time, work harder on those dictional elements that are the least familiar.

Finally, an item that is not a performance technique *per se,* but that is, nevertheless, an exceedingly important part of nearly all readings—the introduction. In practically all cases, the reader must introduce the selection he is going to read. There may be a few instances in which the reader simply walks to the front of the room, or out on the stage, and begins to read with no preparation at all. Certainly such cases are few and very far between. Ordinarily, the reader who faces an audience, no matter what the setting, has the job of getting the audience ready to listen to the thing he is going to read. The one thing that the reader can count on is that the audience will not be ready to listen. This unreadiness may vary all the way from the captive audience (and many classroom audiences are just that) that doesn't want to listen to anything, to the audience that is perfectly willing to listen but doesn't know what to listen for. The all-important thing that the reader has to accomplish in the introduction, the basic purpose of the introduction, is to prepare the audience *emotionally*. Intellectual or factual preparation is, at times, necessary, too, but the emotional preparation is always the primary goal. In effect, an introduction outlines for the audience its emotional duties as a group of listeners. It tells them to get ready to hear, and respond to, sadness or joy or pain. When facts, background materials, etc., are necessary to the audience's emotional response, they must, of course, be included. However, an introduction that is entirely or predominantly factual is a failure, simply because the response that the reader wants from the audience is not an entirely or predominantly intellectual one. The only materials that might be read purely for factual purposes would be minutes of meetings, committee reports, etc., and readers do not ordinarily deal with such material.

The introduction is, in a sense, almost as important as the selection that is read. Certainly many good readings have been complete flops because the introduction didn't work. In preparing the audience emotionally, the reader must relate the attitudes and feelings of the material, of the speaker, to those of the audience. He must say, in some fashion, "We all feel certain things about death, or hate, or anxiety, and here is a selection, a speaker, that expresses just those feelings," or "We all feel certain things about (whatever the subject is), but here is a selection, a speaker, who looks at it differently, whose feelings are rather unusual." It is a matter of pointing out similarities or dissimilarities between the speaker's emotional viewpoint and that of the audience. Notice that, in discussing introductions, the term reader, not reader-speaker, has been used. During the introduction, the reader as a person comes into direct contact with the audience, real or imagined. It is the reader himself that is speaking, and his manner should say quite clearly, "These are my words." When the reading begins, the reader-speaker takes over, direct contact ceases, and the manner of delivery should then indicate equally clearly, "These are the speaker's words."

Here is the sort of introduction that, most emphatically, does not work:

Herbert Q. Steringden, American poet, was born in 1907. He has published four volumes of poetry, the best known of which is *The World's Finest Verse*. The

selection I am going to read is from that work, and is
entitled, "My Verse." "My Verse," by Herbert Q. Steringden. (*Automaton - like step forward.*)

Sample analysis

These comments about performance techniques have been
rather general, and to the student who is looking for rules
and regulations may seem to offer little help. Unfortunately,
to the best of this writer's knowledge, there is no way to give
that sort of help. Instead, an effort will be made to describe
techniques that could be used with a particular selection. It is
a job that has already been admitted to be an impossible one
—that of describing in written language what can be done
with oral language. The selection chosen is fairly difficult in
several ways. It is number LII of a group of poems called
1 x 1 (One Times One), by E. E. Cummings.

Introduction

Historically, lyric poetry was meant to be recited to
music. The word "lyric" is used today to mean the words
of a song. I'd like to read a poem that seems to me to be
half poetry, half music. It's a poem by E. E. Cummings,
and it's about spring and love. In some ways it seems very
modern, but actually it's a traditional song of praise of
love and lovers and spring. In this age of sophistication,
some people seem to think it's a little naïve, or even
corny, and the psychologists may think it's neurotic, to
feel openly and strongly about love. But I imagine most
of us have felt something of the wonder and delight that
this poem expresses. And if we haven't, I think perhaps
we would like to very much.

> "sweet spring is your
> time is my time is our
> time for springtime is lovetime
> and viva sweet love"

(all the merry little birds are
flying in the floating in the
very spirits singing in
are winging in the blossoming)

lovers go and lovers come
awandering awondering
but any two are perfectly
alone there's nobody else alive

(such a sky and such a sun
i never knew and neither did you
and everybody never breathed
quite so many kinds of yes)

not a tree can count his leaves
each herself by opening
but shining who by thousands mean
only one amazing thing

(secretly adoring shyly
tiny winging darting floating
merry in the blossoming
always joyful selves are singing)

"sweet spring is your
time is my time is our
time for springtime is lovetime
and viva sweet love"

As far as meaning is concerned, as far as what the speaker
is saying, this is typical of much of Cummings' poetry. Made
seemingly difficult by unusual syntax and addled (though in
this case only slightly) typography, it is, nonetheless, a conventional poem. There are no words here that are unfamiliar or strange. There are many words that are used in
unfamiliar ways. The key to these uses of words, and to the
poem, is to be found in a statement by Cummings himself:

A poet is somebody who feels, and who expresses his
feeling through words.
This may sound easy. It isn't.

A lot of people think or believe or know they feel—
but that's thinking or believing or knowing; not feeling.
And poetry is feeling—not knowing or believing or thinking.
Almost anybody can learn to think or believe or know,
but not a single human being can be taught to feel. Why?
Because whenever you think or you believe or you
know, you're a lot of other people: but the moment you
feel, you're nobody-but-yourself . . .
As for expressing nobody-but-yourself in words, that
means working just a little harder than anybody who isn't
a poet can possibly imagine. Why? Because nothing is
quite as easy as using words like somebody else. We all
of us do exactly this nearly all of the time—and whenever we do it, we're not poets. . . .

This poem is about feeling, not about "thinking or believing
or knowing." It is about feeling in love in the spring, and the
two things, love and spring, fuse into one. The first stanza
states the case, and the lack of conventional syntax, the running together of "sweet spring," "my time," "your time,"
"our time," and "lovetime," is the first indication of their
oneness.

The second stanza elaborates. "Merry little birds," "flying," and "floating" might refer solely to spring. But "very
spirits singing" brings love back into the picture, and begins
the process of anthropomorphizing spring, making it, not
only a time of love, but a loving time.

The third stanza concentrates on love, and the lovers. It
voices the lovers' ageless belief that no one else has ever really
loved in this incredible way.

The fourth stanza sees spring, or nature, through the
lovers' eyes. Everything becomes new and special. And this
newness and specialness includes even the most ordinary actions of the lovers, each of which means the wonderful,
unbelievable affirmative—"Yes, I love you."

The fifth stanza is nearly all spring. And again an anthro-

pomorphized spring. Spring is peopled by things like trees
(male), whose leaves (female) are numberless and infinitely
different, and yet have one lovely, "shining," and very personal meaning.

The sixth stanza echoes the second. But here the emphasis
is on love. A love that is joyous and that brings the lovers
the same springlike feelings of "winging darting floating/
merry in the blossoming." It is not the "merry little birds"
that behave thus, however, but the "always joyful selves"—
the lovers.

And the song is closed by the chorus—the repeated first
stanza.

An interesting example of Cummings' not "using words
like somebody else" occurs in the fourth stanza. What is the
difference between "everybody never breathed," and "nobody ever breathed"? Surely a difference exists. A difference
in tone or feeling. "Everybody never" is more strangely
emphatic. The lovers are different from "everybody," and
that is different than being different from "nobody."

The over-all meaning of the selection poses no problems.
It is a simple, lyrical theme—the beauty and joy of Love-
Spring. There is no progression of meaning in the sense of
the development of a plot or story line. Instead, the development consists of variations of the basic theme in words that
are used primarily for their poetic value. In other words, it
is one long series of metaphorical and symbolic statements.

What sort of speaker is this? First of all, it is to this reader
a man, but women might easily hear a female voice speaking
here. This speaker is open, expressive; he pours feelings out
in shining streams. He knows love, and accepts its tenderness
and its magic. He is a modern, certainly—the way he uses
language makes that clear. Subjectively, he is emotionally
young—not immature, but young. The setting is only vaguely
indicated; it might be a park, a wood, and it might or might
not include the loved one.

We have, then, a speaker of our own time, probably relatively young, who, in the real or imagined presence of his beloved, expresses with an unusual combination of delicacy and strength his delight in love and the season of love. As to the "how" of the selection, that presents some special problems. This speaker is using verse-poetry. And the rhythm of the material is extraordinarily important. Visually, the thing is deceptive. It looks like it would require two beats to the line, as

> "*sweet* spring is *your* time is
> *my* time is *our* time for,

but that is unworkable. The meaning is thoroughly destroyed. Remember that the line, a visual phenomenon, has no necessary rhythmic value or importance. In this selection, each stanza is a single rhythmic phrase. If it were arranged typographically like this,

> "*sweet* spring is *your* time is *my* time is *our* time for
> *spring*time is *love*time and *viva* sweet *love*,"

it would be less misleading. The italicized syllables are stressed, making for a very regular and familiar pattern, octameter—eight beats, but not to a line, to the rhythmic phrase. There is one important rhythmic change that occurs. The first and last stanzas are dactylic—made up of metrical feet having one stressed and two unstressed syllables (*swéet sp̆rĭng ĭs*). The remaining stanzas are first paeonic. Paeonic is a foot consisting of four syllables, any one of which may be stressed; depending on which syllable is stressed, it is called first, second, third, or fourth paeonic (*Áll thĕ mĕrr̆y lĭttlĕ birds áre / flýĭng ĭn thĕ*). The speaker has made a wise rhythmic choice. The pattern has a lilt that is perfectly suited to the meaning.

In performance, the reader-speaker will pay particular attention to the first and last stanzas, since they set the mood of the piece. He will probably read the first one in a strongly rhythmical fashion, breaking it only to linger a bit longer on "viva." The tempo will be moderate on the first three words, but then will pick up, and the lilting beat will be matched by the use of the upper-middle pitch range and an expression of happiness—a smile of quiet delight, not a broad grin. The reader-speaker may even use just a suggestion of a waltz-like movement—a very, very slight swaying of the head and upper body—to underline the pulsing, lyrical quality. It will be important to read this stanza in a sustained, even fashion. The entire stanza can well be read on a single breath. But if pauses for breath are taken, no hint of a choppy, staccato quality can be allowed.

With the foot change in the second stanza, he will slow the tempo a bit and will be ready for the irregularities in rhythm that occur at several points, especially the first and last lines of the stanza. He will increase the intensity, since this is an elaboration of what has already been said. The feeling will be that this is impossible to say, really, that words can't express it, so listen carefully. The facial expression will change to one of groping, of hunting to find the thing to say, though the smile will remain. The combination of smiling and frowning slightly at the same time—a combination we all use for things inexpressibly happy—will suit the meaning here.

The third stanza changes the mood again. Slightly. This time to a broader praise of all lovers. The intensity is there, but is shown now by a gentleness and tenderness made evident by slowing the tempo still further, lowering the pitch range and the volume, and dropping the frown from the smile-frown combination. The last words will be read with a regard for the rhythm, but more slowly and less evenly than any other words in the selection. It is a drawn out word-group, the "alive" receiving the slight stress that meaning demands, the tempo slowing even further, and the volume trailing off considerably.

The fourth stanza recaptures the personal element. Here it is not "lovers," but "i" and "you." This stanza will be read on a long crescendo, the tempo, intensity, and volume all increasing slightly to express the wonder of the "i"-ness of the whole thing. But the crescendo should halt abruptly before the word "yes." "Yes" should be too delicate, too full of wonder and awe to be uttered with a smile. The smile crumbles and the "yes" means the total surrender of giving, of love.

Then back again to spring, and the fact that even trees mirror this new and magical thing. Again a crescendo, this one uninterrupted, building to the very end, the "one amazing thing" that all the world points to.

And with the sixth stanza another, heightened statement of the mixed-upness of love-lover-spring. Again the intensity rises, the attempt to express what is beyond language. The stanza will be read with more lyric evenness and smoothness than any other. It is one rhythmic and emotional unit. The smile-frown combination comes back. The last words will fade into the final stanza thus solving the stress problem on "singing."

And the refrain. After a very slight pause, as if to say, "Well, it can't be said any better than this," the strongly rhythmical, singing repetition of the first stanza.

Throughout the selection the interpreter will be aware of its lyrical nature. There will be no extreme variations of pitch, volume, intensity, tempo, or movement. Rather, there will be a slight suggestion of chanting, of intoning the words. This is a technique that suits the mood of lyrics and even matches their history and origin. It is a technique that is simple enough, consisting of reading the words in a smooth, flowing manner, rather than choppily or abruptly, and avoiding the extremes just mentioned.

This is not material that calls for exceedingly formal diction, but clarity and precision are important. It is not sloppy or overly conversational. Some practice may be needed in order to maintain the lilting tempo without blurring the diction.

Probably there will be little large-scale movement. Nonspecific, open-hand, searching gestures might be used in several places, but most of the time the movement will be very restrained in scope.

An alert, controlled posture will be maintained throughout the reading. Clearly, no slouching or listless-seeming stance is acceptable with such material.

And, if it all works—if everything fits together—the audience and the reader will experience something of the strange, hurting happiness of love that is this poem.

Conclusion

This, then, is oral interpretation as this writer understands it. As an academic area it is a small one. It's content in terms of history and criticism is not extensive. Nevertheless, there are treasures to be found here for those who mine deeply.

This is a short book. On the following pages will be found a lengthy list of works dealing directly or indirectly with this area. Since this text is not literature in the sense in which that term has been used herein, a word of direct address to the student may be permitted: Read the books in the following list. Read some or all of some or all of them. Let them lead you further into the field. But most important of all, most important by far, read literature itself, whenever and wherever you find it. If any one thing will help you experience fully and deeply literary works, it is the endless and relentless reading of those works. Having read a few dozen pieces of literature leaves you ill-equipped to approach the rest of literature. If you have read hundreds or thousands of selections, you are necessarily armed with a repertoire of critical and appreciative abilities.

Read widely and hungrily. And in the reading, "speak" the literature if you wish to make it your own.

Notes

❦

[1] Northrop Frye, *The Well-Tempered Critic* (Bloomington: Indiana University Press, 1963), pp. 145–150 specifically, but the entire work relates to this concept of literature.

[2] Representative statements regarding the scope of oral interpretation will be found in:
> Otis J. Aggert and Elbert R. Bowen, *Communicative Reading* (New York: Macmillan, 1956). Chloe Armstrong and Paul D. Brandes, *The Oral Interpretation of Literature* (New York: McGraw-Hill, 1963).
> S. H. Clark, *Interpretation of the Printed Page* (New York: Row, Peterson & Co., 1915).
> Martin Cobin, *Theory and Technique of Interpretation* (Englewood Cliffs, N.J.: Prentice-Hall, 1959).
> Wilma H. Grimes and Alethea Smith Mattingly, *Interpretation: Writer, Reader, Audience* (San Francisco: Wadsworth Press, 1961).
> Charlotte Lee, *Oral Interpretation* (Boston: Houghton Mifflin, 1952).

[3] Oral interpretation is defined in terms of performance in all conventional texts in the field. A representative definition will be found in Charlotte Lee, *Oral Interpretation* (Boston: Houghton Mifflin, 1959), pp. 3–7.

[4] Northrop Frye, *op. cit.*, pp. 33–36.

[5] John Ciardi, *How Does a Poem Mean?* (Boston: Houghton Mifflin, 1959), p. 764.

[6] John Ciardi, *op. cit.*, p. 668.

[7] Melville Cane, *Making A Poem* (New York: Harcourt, Brace & World, 1953), p. 23.

[8] W. K. Wimsatt, Jr., *The Verbal Icon* (New York: Noonday Press, 1958), Chap. 1.

⁹ This point is made most clearly and convincingly by Don Geiger, *The Sound, Sense, and Performance of Literature* (Palo Alto, Calif.: Scott, Foresman and Company, 1963), especially Chap. 6, and Cleanth Brooks, *The Well-Wrought Urn* (New York: Harcourt, Brace & World, 1947), especially Chap. 1.

¹⁰ Don Geiger, *The Sound, Sense, and Performance of Literature* (Palo Alto, Calif.: Scott, Foresman and Company, 1963), p. 4.

¹¹ Wilma H. Grimes and Alethea Smith Mattingly, *Interpretation: Writer, Reader, Audience* (San Francisco: Wadsworth Press, 1961), p. 61.

¹² W. K. Wimsatt, Jr., *loc. cit.*

¹³ John Ciardi, *op. cit.*, pp. 802–803.

¹⁴ Susanne K. Langer, *Philosophy in a New Key* (New York: Mentor Books, 1948), especially Chap. 2 and 3.

¹⁵ For a lengthier discussion of this view of metaphor and symbolism see Paul N. Campbell, *Oral Interpretation* (New York: Macmillan, 1966), Chap. 1.

¹⁶ Paul N. Campbell, *op. cit.*, Chap. 3, offers an expanded treatment of this concept, as does Francis A. Cartier, "Three Misconceptions of Communication," *ETC., A Review of General Semantics*, Vol. XX, No. 2 (July 1963), pp. 135–145.

¹⁷ This idea is stressed by all semanticists. Their major source idea is Alfred Korzybski, *Science and Sanity* (4th ed.) (Lakeville, Conn.: The International Non-Aristotelian Library Publishing Company, 1958), especially Part VII.

¹⁸ For a more detailed discussion of poetry, nonpoetry, prose, verse, and rhythm, see Paul N. Campbell, *op. cit.*, Chap. 1 and 2.

¹⁹ The distinction between verse and poetry has been made by writers dating all the way from Aristotle in *The Poetics*, to Northrop Frye, *op. cit.*, and John Dolman, Jr., *The Art of Reading Aloud* (New York: Harper & Row, 1956), especially Chap. 4.

²⁰ For a study of the various verse rhythms and their relation to written language, see Paul N. Campbell, *op. cit.*, Chap. 2, and the contrasting but similar approach of John Dolman, Jr., *The Art of Reading Aloud* (New York: Harper & Row, 1956), especially Chap. 4, 5, and 7.

²¹ The author was first introduced to this schematic device in the classes of Professor Frank Baxter at the University of Southern California.

²² Elizabeth Drew, *Poetry* (New York: Dell, 1959), p. 36.

²³ *Ibid.*

²⁴ See, for example, Wilma H. Grimes and Alethea Smith Mattingly, *op. cit.*

²⁵ Northrop Frye, *op. cit.*, p. 121.

[26] Don Geiger, *op. cit.*, pp. 77–78.

[27] Eric Berne, *Transactional Analysis in Psychotherapy* (New York: Grove Press, 1961), p. 21.

[28] James A. Michener, *Hawaii* (New York: Bantam Books, 1961), p. 1.

[29] Elizabeth Drew, *op. cit.*, Chap. 2, and Elizabeth Drew, *Discovering Poetry* (New York: W. W. Norton & Co., 1933), pp. 47–69.

[30] Aristotle, *The Poetics*, Chap. 1–5.

[31] Charlotte Lee, *op. cit.*, Chap. 1.

[32] For representative attitudes toward the use of techniques by the interpreter, see:
Samual Silas Curry, *Foundations of Expression* (Boston, 1920).
Otis J. Aggert and Elbert R. Bowen, *Communicative Reading* (New York: Macmillan, 1956).
Wilma H. Grimes and Alethea Smith Mattingly, *op. cit.*

[33] Samual Silas Curry, *Foundations of Expression* (Boston, 1920), especially Chap. 7.

Bibliography

❦

GENERAL THEORY AND CRITICISM, SEMANTICS, AESTHETICS, AND
LITERARY CRITICISM

Abrams, M. H., *The Mirror and the Lamp*, New York, 1953.
Aldridge, J. W., ed., *Critiques and Essays in Modern Fiction,
1920–1951*, New York, 1952.
Alexander, Samuel, *Beauty and Other Forms of Value*, London,
1933.
Aristotle, *Aristotle's Theory of Poetry and Fine Art*, trans.
S. H. Butcher, New York, 1951.
Bate, Walter J., ed., *Criticism: The Major Texts*, New York,
1948.
Baum, Paull F., *The Principles of English Versification*,
Cambridge, Mass., 1922.
————, *The Other Harmony of Prose*, Durham, N.C., 1952.
Beardsley, Monroe C., *Aesthetics: Problems in the Philosophy
of Criticism*, New York, 1958.
Bergson, Henri, *The Creative Mind*, trans. Mabelle L. Andison,
New York, 1946.
————, *Philosophy of Poetry*, trans. Wade Baskin, New York,
1959.
Blakmur, Richard P., *Language as Gesture, Essays in Poetry*,
New York, 1952.
————, *The Lion and the Honeycomb*, New York, 1955.
Bloom, Edward A., Charles H. Philbrick, and Elmer M. Blistein,
The Order of Poetry, New York, 1961.

149

Bode, Carl, ed., *The Great Experiment in American Literature*, New York, 1961.

Booth, Wayne C., *The Rhetoric of Fiction*, Chicago, 1961.

Bowers, Fredson, *Textual and Literary Criticism*, New York, 1959.

Brooks, Cleanth, *Modern Poetry and the Tradition*, Chapel Hill, N.C., 1939.

————, *The Well-Wrought Urn*, New York, 1947.

————, and R. P. Warren, *Understanding Poetry*, New York, 1938.

————, *Understanding Fiction*, New York, 1943.

Brower, Reuben A., *The Fields of Light. An Experiment in Critical Reading*, New York, 1951.

Burke, Kenneth, *A Grammar of Motives*, Englewood Cliffs, N.J., 1945.

————, *The Philosophy of Literary Form: Studies in Symbolic Action*, New York, 1957.

Burnshaw, Stanley, ed., *The Poem Itself*, New York, 1960.

Cane, Melville, *Making A Poem*, New York, 1953.

Caudwell, Christopher, *Illusion and Reality*, London, 1937.

Cherry, Colin, *On Human Communication: A Review, a Survey, and a Criticism*, New York, 1957.

Ciardi, John, *How Does A Poem Mean?*, Boston, 1959.

————, ed., *Mid-Century American Poets*, New York, 1950.

Coffman, G. C., *Studies and Language of Literature*, Chapel Hill, N.C., 1945.

Crane, Ronald S., *The Languages of Criticism and the Structure of Poetry*, Toronto, 1953.

————, "Literature, Philosophy and Ideas," *Modern Philology*, LII (1954), pp. 78–83.

Crowl, Morris W., "The Cadence of English Oratorical Prose," *Studies in Philology*, XVI (1919), pp. 1–55.

Dabney, I. P., *The Musical Basis of Verse*, New York, 1901.

Daiches, David, *Literature and Society*, London, 1938.

————, *The Novel and the Modern World*, Chicago, 1939.

————, *Poetry and the Modern World*, Chicago, 1940.

————, *A Study of Literature*, Ithaca, N.Y., 1948.

————, *Critical Approaches to Literature*, Englewood Cliffs, N.J., 1956.

Davie, Donald, *Purity of Diction in English Verse*, New York, 1953.

Day-Lewis, Cecil, *The Poetic Image*, New York, 1948.

Dearing, Vinton A., *A Manual of Textual Analysis*, Los Angeles, 1959.

Deutsch, Babette, *Poetry Handbook: A Dictionary of Terms*, New York, 1957.

Dewey, John, *Art as Experience*, New York, 1934.

Drew, Elizabeth, *Discovering Poetry*, New York, 1933.

————, *Poetry*, New York, 1959.

Duncan, Hugh Dalziel, *Language and Literature in Society*, Chicago, 1953.

Eastman, Max, *The Literary Mind*, New York, 1931.

Ehrenpreis, Irwin, *The "Types" Approach to Literature*, New York, 1945.

Eliot, T. S., *The Use of Poetry and the Use of Criticism*, Cambridge, Mass., 1933.

————, *Poetry and Drama*, Cambridge, Mass., 1951.

Empson, William, *Seven Types of Ambiguity*, London, 1930 (new ed., New York, 1948; Penguin Books, 1962).

Feidelson, Charles, Jr., *Symbolism and American Literature*, Chicago, 1953.

Foerster, Norman, John C. McGalliard, René Wellek, Austin Warren, and Wilber Lang Schramm, *Literary Scholarship: Its Aims and Methods*, Chapel Hill, N.C., 1941.

Foss, Martin, *Symbol and Metaphor in Human Experience*, Princeton, N.J., 1949.

Foster, Richard, *The New Romantics: A Reappraisal of the New Criticism*, Bloomington, Ind., 1962.

Friedman, Norman, "Imagery: From Sensation to Symbol," *Journal of Aesthetics*, XII (1953), pp. 24–37.

Frye, Northrop, *Anatomy of Criticism: Four Essays*, Princeton, N.J., 1957.

————, ed., *Sound and Poetry*, New York, 1957.

————, *The Well-Tempered Critic*, Bloomington, Ind., 1963.

Gardiner, Alan H., *The Theory of Speech and Language*, New York, 1932.

Garnett, A. C., *Reality and Value*, New Haven, Conn., 1937.

Ghiselin, Brewster, ed., *The Creative Process: A Symposium*, New York, 1955.

Goodman, Paul, *The Structure of Literature*, Chicago, 1954.

Greene, Theodore Meyer, *The Arts and the Art of Criticism*, Princeton, N.J., 1940.

Guérard, Albert L., *A Preface to World Literature*, New York, 1940.

Hamm, Victor M., "Meter and Meaning," *PMLA*, LXIX (1954), pp. 695–710.

Harap, Louis, "What Is Poetic Truth?", *Journal of Philosophy*, XXX (1933), pp. 477–88.

Hatzfeld, Halmut, "The Language of the Poet," *Studies in Philology*, XLIII (1946), pp. 93–120.

Hayakawa, S. I., *Language in Thought and Action*, New York, 1949.

Holloway, John, *The Chartered Mirror. Literary and Critical Essays*, London, 1960.

Hospers, John, *Meaning and Truth in the Arts*, Chapel Hill, N.C., 1946.

Hungerford, Edward, *Shores of Darkness*, New York, 1941.

Hungerland, Isabel C., *Poetic Discourse*, Berkeley, Calif., 1958.

Hyman, Stanley Edgar, *The Armed Vision: A Study in the Methods of Modern Literary Criticism*, New York, 1948.

Isaacs, J., *The Background of Modern Poetry*, New York, 1958.

Jacob, Cary T., *The Foundation and Nature of Verse*, New York, 1918.

James, Henry, *The Art of Fiction*, New York, 1948.

Jarrell, Randall, *Poetry and The Age*, New York, 1955.

Jesperson, Otto, *Growth and Structure of the English Language*, New York, 1955.

Jones, Howard Mumford, *The Theory of American Literature*, Cambridge, Mass., 1949.

Kern, Alexander C., "The Sociology of Knowledge in the Study of Literature," *Sewanee Revue*, L (1942), pp. 505–14.

Koestler, Arthur, *The Act of Creation*, New York, 1964.

Krieger, Murray, *The New Apologists for Poetry*, Minneapolis, 1957.

Laird, John, *The Idea of Value*, Cambridge, England, 1929.

Lalo, Charles, "The Aesthetic Analysis of a Work of Art: An Essay on the Structure and the Superstructure of Poetry," *Journal of Aesthetics*, VII (1949), pp. 278–93.

Langer, Susanne K., *Philosophy in a New Key: A Study in the*

Symbolism of Reason, Rite, and Art, Cambridge, Mass., 1942.

————, *Feeling and Form. A Theory of Art Developed from Philosophy in a New Key*, New York, 1953.

Lanier, Sidney, *Science of English Verse*, New York, 1880 (new ed. with introduction by P. F. Baum in *Centennial Edition*, ed. Charles Anderson, Baltimore 1945, Vol. II, pp. vii–xlviii).

Lanz, Henry, *The Physical Basis of Rime: An Essay on the Aesthetics of Sound*, Stanford, Calif., 1931.

Leavis, F. R., "The Literary Discipline and Liberal Education," *Sewanee Revue*, LV (1947) pp. 586–609.

Levin, Harry, *Contexts of Criticism*, New York, 1963.

Miles, Josephine, *The Vocabulary of Poetry*, Berkeley, Calif., 1946.

————, *The Continuity of Poetic Language*, Berkeley, Calif., 1951.

Moulton, R. G., *The Modern Study of Literature*, Chicago, 1915.

Murray, Gilbert, *The Classical Tradition in Poetry*, New York, 1957.

Norman, Charles, ed., *Poets on Poetry*, New York, 1962.

Nowottny, Winifred, *The Language Poets Use*, New York, 1962.

O'Connor, William V., ed., *Forms of Modern Fiction*, Minneapolis, 1948.

————, *Sense and Sensibility in Modern Poetry*, Chicago, 1948.

Ogden, C. K., and I. A. Richards, *The Meaning of Meaning: A Study of the Influence of Language Upon Thought and of the Science of Symbolism*, London, 1923; 7th ed., New York, 1945.

Osborne, Harold, *Aesthetics and Criticism*, London, 1955.

Peacock, Ronald, *The Poet in the Theater*, New York, 1946.

Pei, Mario, *The Story of Language*, Philadelphia, 1949.

————, *The Story of English*, Philadelphia, 1952.

Pell, Orlie A., *Value-Theory and Criticism*, New York, 1930.

Pepper, Stephen, *The Basis of Criticism in the Arts*, Cambridge, Mass., 1945.

————, ed., *The Creative Process: A Symposium*, New York, 1955.

Perrine, Laurence, *Sound and Sense: An Introduction to Poetry*, New York, 1956.

Perry, Ralph B., *General Theory of Value*, New York, 1926.

Peyre, Henri, *Writers and Their Critics*, Ithaca, N.Y., 1944.

Pike, Kenneth L., *The Intonation of American English*, Ann Arbor, Mich., 1947.

Pollock, Thomas C., *The Nature of Literature*, Princeton, N.J., 1942.

Potter, Stephen, *The Muse in Chains: A Study in Education*, London, 1937.

Pottle, Frederick A., *The Idiom of Poetry*, Ithaca, N.Y., 1941; new enlarged ed., 1946.

Prescott, Frederick C., *Poetry and Myth*, New York, 1927.

Rank, Otto, *Art and Artist*, New York, 1932.

Ransom, John Crowe, *The World's Body*, New York, 1938.

————, "The Pragmatics of Art," *Kenyon Revue*, II (1940), pp. 76–87.

————, *The New Criticism*, Norfolk, Conn., 1941.

Read, Herbert, *Art and Society*, London, 1937.

————, *The Nature of Literature*, New York, n.d.

Reid, John R., *A Theory of Value*, New York, 1938.

Rice, Philip Blair, "Quality and Value," *Journal of Philosophy*, XL (1943), pp. 337–48.

Richards, I. A., *Principles of Literary Criticism*, London, 1924.

————, *Practical Criticism*, New York, 1929.

Roellinger, R. X., Jr., "Two Theories of Poetry As Knowledge," *Southern Revue*, VII (1942), pp. 690–705.

Sanders, George, *A Poetry Primer*, New York, 1935.

Sapir, Edward, *Language*, New York, 1921.

Sebeok, Thomas A., ed., *Style in Language*, New York, 1960.

Sewell, Elizabeth, *The Structure of Poetry*, New York, 1952.

Shepard, William, "Recent Theories of Textual Criticism," *Modern Philology*, XXVIII (1930), pp. 129–41.

Shumaker, Wayne, *Elements of Critical Theory*, Berkeley, Calif., 1952.

Skelton, Robin, *The Poetic Pattern*, London, 1956.

Smith, Chard Powers, *Pattern and Variation in Poetry*, New York, 1932.

Smith, James Harry, and Edd Winfield Parks, eds., *The Great Critics: An Anthology of Literary Criticism*, New York, 1951.

Spitzer, Leo, *Linguistics and Literary History: Essays in Stylistics*, Princeton, N.J., 1948.

Stallman, R. W., ed., *Critiques and Essays in Criticism, 1920–1948*, New York, 1949.

Stauffer, Donald, *The Nature of Poetry*, New York, 1946.

Stevenson, Charles L., *Ethics and Language*, New Haven, Conn., 1944.

Tate, Allen, ed., *The Language of Poetry*, Princeton, N.J., 1942.

——————, *On the Limits of Poetry; Selected Essays: 1928–1948*, New York, 1948.

Thompson, John, *The Founding of English Metre*, London, 1961.

Trilling, Lionel, "The Meaning of a Literary Idea," *The Liberal Imagination*, New York, 1950, pp. 281–303.

Valéry, Paul, *The Art of Poetry*, trans. Denise Folliott, New York, 1958.

Vivas, Eliseo, "The Esthetic Judgment," *Journal of Philosophy*, XXXIII (1936), pp. 57–69.

——————, "A Note on Value," *Journal of Philosophy*, XXXIII (1936), pp. 568–75.

Walsh, Dorothy, "The Cognitive Content of Art," *Philosophical Revue*, LII (1943), pp. 433–51.

Wells, Henry W., *Poetic Imagery*, New York, 1948.

West, Ray B., Jr., ed., *Essays in Modern Literary Criticism*, New York, 1952.

Wharton, Edith, *The Writing of Fiction*, New York, 1924.

Wheelwright, Philip, "On the Semantics of Poetry," *Kenyon Revue*, II (1940), pp. 263–83.

——————, *Metaphor and Reality*, Bloomington, Ind., 1962.

Whitcomb, Seldon L., *The Study of a Novel*, Boston, 1905.

Whiteford, R. N., *Motives in English Fiction*, New York, 1918.

Williamson, George, *The Senecan Amble. A Story of Prose Form from Bacon to Collier*, Chicago, 1951.

Wilson, Katherine M., *Sound and Meaning in English Poetry*, London, 1930.

Wimsatt, William K., Jr., *The Verbal Icon: Studies in the Meaning of Poetry*, Lexington, Ky., 1954.

————, and M. C. Beardsley, "The Concept of Meter: An Exercise in Abstraction," *PMLA*, LXXIV (1959), pp. 585–98.

————, and Cleanth Brooks, *Literary Criticism: A Short History*, New York, 1957.

Winters, Yvor, *In Defense of Reason*, Denver, 1947.

Witte, W., "The Sociological Approach to Literature," *Modern Philology*, LII (1954), pp. 78–83.

PSYCHOLOGY AND PSYCHOLOGICAL APPROACHES TO LITERATURE

Allers, Rudolph, *The Psychology of Character*, New York, 1943.

Allport, Gordon W., and Philip E. Vernon, *Studies in Expressive Movement*, New York, 1933.

Arnheim, Rudolph, *et al.*, *Poets at Work*, New York, 1948.

Basler, Roy P., *Sex, Symbolism and Psychology in Literature*, New Brunswick, N.J., 1948.

Bergler, Edmond, *The Writer and Psychoanalysis*, New York, 1950.

Burke, Kenneth, "Freud and the Analysis of Poetry," *Philosophy of Literary Form*, Baton Rouge, La., 1941, pp. 258–92.

Chandler, Albert R., *Beauty and Human Nature: Elements of Psychological Aesthetics*, New York, 1934.

Davies, Robert Gorham, "Art and Anxiety," *Partisan Revue*, XIV (1945), pp. 310–21.

de Vries, Louis Peter, *The Nature of Poetic Literature*, Seattle, 1930.

Downey, June, *Creative Imagination*, London, 1929.

Dunbar, Helen Flanders, *Emotions and Bodily Changes*, New York, 1954.

Efron, David, *Gesture and Environment*, New York, 1941.

Frank, Lawrence K., *Feelings and Emotions*, New York, 1954.

Friedman, Melvin J., *Stream of Consciousness: A Study in Literary Method*, New Haven, Conn., 1955.

Grigson, Geoffrey, ed., *The Arts Today*, London, 1935.

Hargreaves, H. L., "The 'Faculty' of Imagination," *British Journal of Psychology, Monograph Supplement*, III (1927).

Hill, J. C., "Poetry and the Unconscious," *British Journal of Medical Psychology*, IV (1924), pp. 125–33.

Hyman, Stanley E., "The Psychoanalytical Criticism of Literature," *Western Revue*, XII (1947–48), pp. 106–15.

Jung, Carl Gustav, *Man and His Symbols*, Garden City, N.Y., 1964.

Kris, Ernst, *Psychoanalytic Explorations in Art*, New York, 1952.

Lesser, Simon O., *Fiction and the Unconscious*, Boston, 1957.

Lewis, C. S., "Psychoanalysis and Literary Criticism," *Essays and Studies of the English Association*, XXVII (1941), pp. 7–21.

Lucas, F. L., *Literature and Psychology*, London, 1951.

Maritain, Jacques, *Creative Intuition in Art and Poetry*, New York, 1953.

Munro, Thomas, "Methods in the Psychology of Art," *Journal of Aesthetics*, VI (1948), pp. 225–35.

Niebuhr, Reinhold, *The Self and the Dramas of History*, New York, 1955.

Perky, C. W., "An Experimental Study of Imagination," *American Journal of Psychology*, XXI (1910), pp. 422–52.

Reik, Theodor, *The Secret Self; Psychoanalytic Experiences in Life and Literature*, New York, 1952.

Ruesch, Jurgen, and Weldon Kees, *Nonverbal Communication*, Berkeley, Calif., 1956.

Sachs, Hanns, *Creative Unconscious*, Cambridge, Mass., 1951.

Sartre, Jean-Paul, *The Emotions: Outline of a Theory*, New York, 1948.

Stekel, Wilhelm, "Poetry and Neurosis," *Psychoanalytic Revue*, X (1923), pp. 73–96, 190–208, 316–28, 457–66.

Trilling, Lionel, "A Note on Art and Neurosis," *Partisan Revue*, XII (1945), pp. 41–9.

Tsanoff, Radoslav A., "On the Psychology of Poetic Construction," *American Journal of Psychology*, XXV (1914), pp. 528–37.

Wolff, Charlotte, *A Psychology of Gesture*, London, 1948.

Oral Interpretation

Armstrong, Chloe, and Paul D. Brandes, *The Oral Interpretation of Literature*, New York, 1963.

Austin, Gilbert, *Chironomia; or a Treatise on (Rhetorical) De-

livery: Comprehending Many Precepts Both Ancient and Modern, for the Proper Regulation of the Voice, the Countenance and Gesture, London, 1806.

Bacon, Albert M., *A Manual of Gesture*, New York, 1893.

Bacon, Wallace A., and Robert S. Breen, *Literature as Experience*, New York, 1959.

Barber, Jonathan, *Exercises in Reading and Recitation*, York, Pa., 1825.

————, *A Grammar of Elocution*, New Haven, Conn., 1830.

Bassett, Lee Emerson, *Handbook of Oral Reading*, Boston, 1917.

Bell, Alexander Melville, *The Principles of Elocution*, New York, 1887.

Blair, Hugh, *Lectures on Rhetoric and Belles Lettres*, London, n.d.

Bronson, C. P., *Elocution; or Mental and Vocal Philosophy: Involving the Principles of Reading and Speaking; and Designed for the Development and Cultivation of Both Body and Mind, in Accordance with the Nature, Uses, and Destiny of Man*, Louisville, Ky., 1845.

Bulwer, John, *Chirologia . . . Chironomia*, London, 1644.

Burgh, James, *The Art of Speaking, Containing an Essay in Which Are Given Rules for Expressing Properly the Principal Passions and Humors, Which Occur in Reading, or Public Speaking, Taken from the Ancients and Moderns; Exhibiting A Variety of Matter for Practice; the Emphatical Words Printed in Italics; with Notes of Direction Referring to the Essay*, Baltimore, 1804.

Caldwell, Merritt, *A Practical Manual of Elocution*, Philadelphia, 1845.

Campbell, Hugh, R. F. Brewer, and Henry Neville, *Voice, Speech and Gesture: Practical Handbook to the Elocutionary Art*, New York, 1895.

Campbell, Paul N., *Oral Interpretation*, New York, 1966.

Chamberlain, William B., and Solomon H. Clark, *Principles of Vocal Expression*, Chicago, 1897.

Clark, Solomon H., *Interpretation of the Printed Page*, New York, 1915.

Cobin, Martin, *Theory and Technique of Interpretation*, Englewood Cliffs, N.J., 1959.

Comstock, Andrew, *A System of Elocution*, Philadelphia, 1851.

Cooper, Charles W., *Preface to Poetry*, New York, 1946.

Corson, Hiram, *The Voice and Spiritual Education*, New York, 1897.

Crocker, Lionel, *Interpretative Speech*, New York, 1952.

——, and Louis M. Eich, *Oral Reading*, New York, 1955.

Cunningham, Cornelius Carman, *Literature as a Fine Art*, New York, 1941.

Curry, Samuel Silas, *The Province of Expression*, Boston, 1891.

——, *Imagination and the Dramatic Instinct*, Boston, 1896.

——, *Foundations of Expression*, Boston, 1907.

——, *Mind and Voice*, Boston, 1910.

Delaumosne, l'Abbé, "The Delsarte System," *The Delsarte System of Oratory*, New York, 1893.

Diehl, Anna Randall, *A Practical Delsarte Primer*, Syracuse, N.Y., 1890.

Dolman, John, Jr., *The Art of Reading Aloud*, New York, 1956.

Dwyer, John H., *An Essay on Elocution*, New York, 1828.

Fulton, Robert I., and Thomas C. Trueblood, *Practical Elements of Elocution*, Boston, 1898.

Geiger, Don, *The Sound, Sense, and Performance of Literature*, Palo Alto, Calif., 1963.

Hargis, Donald, "What Is Oral Interpretation?", *Western Speech*, XVI (1952), pp. 175–80.

——, "Interpretation as Oral Communication," *Central States Speech Journal*, XI (1960), pp. 168–73.

Johnson, Gertrude E., ed., *Studies in the Art of Interpretation*, New York, 1940.

Kerfoot, John B., *How to Read*, Boston, 1916.

Lee, Charlotte I., *Oral Interpretation*, Boston, 1965.

Lowrey, Sara, and Gertrude E. Johnson, *Interpretative Reading: Techniques and Selections*, New York, 1953.

McIlvaine, Joshua H., *Elocution: The Sources and Elements of Its Power*, New York, 1870.

McLean, Margaret P., *Oral Interpretation of Forms of Literature*, New York, 1936.

Mandeville, Henry, *The Elements of Reading and Oratory*, New York, 1887.

Murdoch, James E., *A Plea for Spoken Language*, New York, 1883.

——, *Analytic Elocution*, New York, 1884.

Northrop, Henry Davenport, *The Delsarte Speaker,* Philadelphia, 1895.

Palmer, Erastus, and L. Walter Sammis, *The Principles of Oral English,* New York, 1906.

Parrish, Wayland Maxfield, *Reading Aloud,* New York, 1932.

Porter, Ebenezer, *The Rhetorical Reader,* New York, 1835.

————, *Analysis of Principles of Rhetorical Delivery as Applied in Reading and Speaking,* Andover, Mass., 1836.

Robb, Mary Margaret, *Oral Interpretation of Literature in American Colleges and Universities,* New York, 1941.

Rush, James, *The Philosophy of the Human Voice,* Philadelphia, 1855.

Russell, William, *The American Elocutionist,* Boston, 1854.

Sarett, Lew, and William Trufant Foster, *Basic Principles of Speech,* Boston, 1936.

Sheridan, Thomas, *Lectures on the Art of Reading,* London, 1775.

————, *A Rhetorical Grammar of the English Language,* Dublin, 1781.

————, *Course of Lectures on Elocution,* London, 1796.

Shurter, Edwin DuBois, *Public Speaking, A Treatise on Delivery with Selections for Declaiming,* Boston, 1903.

Smith, Joseph F., and James R. Linn, *Skill in Reading Aloud,* New York, 1960.

Stebbins, Genevieve, *Delsarte System of Dramatic Expression,* New York, 1886.

Steele, Joshua, *Prosodia Rationalis, An Essay Towards Establishing the Melody and Measure of Speech To Be Expressed and Perpetuated by Peculiar Symbols,* London, 1775.

Tallcott, Rollo Anson, *The Art of Acting and Public Reading,* Indianapolis, 1922.

Thompson, David W., and Virginia Fredericks, *Oral Interpretation of Fiction,* Minneapolis, 1964.

Tressider, Argus, *Reading to Others,* New York, 1940.

Walker, John, *The Melody of Speaking Delineated, or Elocution Taught Like Music by Visible Signs,* London, 1787.

————, *Elements of Elocution,* Boston, 1810.

————, *The Rhetorical Grammar,* Boston, 1814.

Woolbert, Charles H., and Severina E. Nelson, *The Art of Interpretative Speech,* New York, 1929.

Index

❦